A Beginners Guide to Christian Prepping and Prayer:

Learn How to Prepare You and Your Family for SHTF, Natural Disasters, Civil Unrest, Economic Collapse, an EMP Strike, and other Apocalyptic Events of the End Times while Remaining Fervent in Prayer

By: Tom Eckerd

Copyright © 2017
American Christian Defense Alliance, Inc.
Baltimore, Maryland

ACDAINC.ORG

All Rights Reserved. No part of this publication may be reproduced in any form or by any means, including scanning, photocopying, or otherwise without prior written permission of the copyright holder.

Special Request

Thank you for purchasing our book and supporting our Ministry. We actually have two requests – To Pray for Our Ministry and to Read this Book All the Way through. No Ministry can survive without Prayer and Support so we ask you to keep our Ministry in Your Daily Prayers and Pray as the Lord leads.

We encourage you to Read the Book you purchased all the way through. Many Books NEVER Get Read, and the ones that do only get read the first few pages.

One of our Special Request is that if you are serious about learning the material in this book that you take time to actually read this book in its entirety – all the way through.

We all lead such busy lives nowadays and can get side tracked so easily please take a moment to consider my words and read to the end of the book and keep us in Your Prayers.

Thank You once again for purchase. We deeply appreciate Your Prayers and Support and know that God will Bless You as You continue to Bless this Ministry.

Dedication

This Book is dedicated to All the Christian Patriot Prayer Warriors out there who Stand in the Gap for their Family, their Faith, and for Freedom

God Bless Each of You

Forward

This book, "A Beginners Guide to Christian Prepping and Prayer" is a combination of three of our books, "Christian Prepping 101", Biblical Bug Out and "Prayer" We have created this bundle to give you an all-inclusive book to reference when searching for answers regarding Christian Prepping and Prayer.

If you're looking for solid answers for how to get started strengthening your Prayer Life and Prepping as a Christian this book is for you. This book has the answers to what God's plan is and has been for his people this book is a must and how critical Prayer is to Your Daily Life.

We look forward to seeing you on the inside and welcome your feedback.

Table of Contents

Special Request 2

Dedication 4

Forward 5

Christian Prepping 101:How To Start Prepping . 11

Special Request 12

Dedication 14

Forward 15

Chapter 1: 17

What is Christian Prepping 17

Chapter 2: Understand the Why 26

Chapter 3: Spiritual Survival 33

Chapter 4: What is God's Plan 38

Chapter 5: Educating Yourself 42

Chapter 6: 47

Five Foundations of Survival 47

Chapter 7: How to Start Prepping 71

Chapter 8: Kits & Bags 104

Chapter 9: The EDC 110

Chapter 10: The Bug Out Bag 116

Chapter 11: The INCH Bag 121

Chapter 12: The Bug Out Vehicle (BOV) 126

Chapter 13: The Bug Out Retreat (BOR) 130

Chapter 14: Caching 134

Chapter 15: Alternative Housing Options 140

Chapter 16: Alternative Energy Options 142

Chapter 17: What to Buy 147

Chapter 18: Personal Care 151

Conclusion 154

Special Gift 157

Stay In Contact 159

Find All Our Books 160

Biblical Bug Out: Don't Bug In - Follow the Calling 162

Special Request 163

Dedication 165

Forward 166

Chapter 1: Is Bugging Out Really God's Plan? 168

Chapter 2: Why Bug Out? 178

Chapter 3: Spiritual Awareness 182

Chapter 4: How to Start Your Bug-Out Preparations 190

Chapter 5: Where Do I Go? 195

Chapter 6: How Do I Get There? 200

Chapter 7: What to Do When There? 205

Chapter 8: The Bug Out Bag 212

Chapter 9: Creating Supply Caches 221

Chapter 10: Financial Considerations 226

Chapter 11: Get Off the Grid 231

Chapter 12: Considerations for Families .. 238

Chapter 13: Conclusion 244

Special Gift 247

Stay In Contact 249

Find All Our Books 250

Prayer 252

Disclaimer 253

Special Request 255

Dedication 257

Forward 258

Chapter 1: What is Prayer? 260

Chapter 2: How to Pray 271

Chapter 3: Why Pray 282

Chapter 4: Making Time to Pray 289

Chapter 5: Praying the Scriptures 298

Chapter 6: Praying for God's Will to be Done 305

Chapter 7: Jesus Example of Prayer 308

Chapter 8: Learning to be a Warrior 325

Chapter 9: Praying for Healing 339

Chapter 10: Praying as a Means of Spiritual Warfare 346

Chapter 11: Developing Your List 358

Chapter 12: When It Seems God Doesn't Hear Your Prayers 365

Chapter 13: Fasting and Prayer 369

Chapter 14: Conclusion 391

Special Gift 395

Stay In Contact 397

Find All Our Books 398

Christian Prepping 101:
How To Start Prepping

By: Tom Eckerd

All Rights Reserved. No part of this publication may be reproduced in any form or by any means, including scanning, photocopying, or otherwise without prior written permission of the copyright holder.

Copyright © 2016
American Christian Defense Alliance, Inc.
Baltimore, Maryland

ACDAInc.Org

Special Request

Thank you for purchasing our book and supporting our Ministry. We actually have two requests – To Pray for Our Ministry and to Read this Book All the Way through. No Ministry can survive without Prayer and Support so we ask you to keep our Ministry in Your Daily Prayers and Pray as the Lord leads.

We encourage you to Read the Book you purchased all the way through. Many Books NEVER Get Read, and the ones that do only get read the first few pages.

One of our Special Request is that if you are serious about learning the material in this book that you take time to actually read this book in its entirety – all the way through.

We all lead such busy lives nowadays and can get side tracked so easily please take a moment to consider my words and read to the end of the book and keep us in Your Prayers.

Thank You once again for purchase. We deeply appreciate Your Prayers and Support and know that God will Bless You as You continue to Bless this Ministry.

Dedication

This book is dedicated to the watchmen of God who faithfully watch and pray as Lord commanded all of us to do and to my Lord and Savior Jesus Christ who continues to lead, guide and protect us as we move forward in courage and faith to shine the light into the darkness.

Forward

This book is a follow-up to our previous book, Biblical Bug Out: Don't Bug In - Follow The Calling. In the previous book we discussed the concept of bugging out and indicated through Scripture how this was a Biblical principle. We felt compelled in our spirit, given the lateness of the hour to put out that book first to provide immediate solutions to Christians looking for answers in dark times.

In this book we laid the foundations of what we consider to be "Christian Prepping". If you're a Christian and into prepping you should enjoy this book as a gives a clear concise systematic approach to prepping from a Christian perspective. We have attempted to touch on all of the critical items one should consider when seeking to be prepared. For many Christian Preppers just starting out this may in fact end up being your go to book as you prepare you and your family for what's to come.

Preppers in general have many reasons for preparing - Some see economic collapse on the horizon, some see an EMP detonated over the United States knocking on the power grid, others may see cyber terrorism infecting the majority of computers and infrastructure of the United States, still yet others may see a World War III scenario taking place - Preppers have so many things they are preparing for. However, the Christian Prepper may have less to consider or more to consider depending upon how you look at things. One thing is for certain the Christian Prepper is unique within the prepping community as their focus for it centers on Jesus Christ and the events leading to His imminent return.

Start your journey now by reading this book and gaining necessary insight on how you and your family can be truly prepared.

Chapter 1:
What is Christian Prepping

What is Christian prepping some might ask. Christian prepping can be defined as prepping based off of prophecy and the Word of God. In the Word of God we can find many examples of various men and women of faith who God warned of things to come and enabled them to prepare. In today's modern times God still operates the same way, He still warns his people of the dangers to come – both physical dangers as well spiritual dangers. Christian prepping combines both aspects to enable the believer to prepare fully for what's to come.

One of the fundamental differences of Christian prepping versus just prepping is that Christian prepping is centered around a belief, a passion and a sincere desire to put Jesus Christ first and foremost in everything we do

– it is the fact that we prep not out of fear of what is to come or what may come but a genuine love for our families and those around us - knowing that in a time of need, a time of crisis we must stand in the gap and be prepared.

For the Christian Prepper their greatest prep, their greatest asset rather is the Holy Spirit, the Word of God and as I mentioned before Jesus Christ. To the Christian Prepper it's not about stuff that we may acquire to deal with a particular situation or scenario. Having these things are great but if you don't have Christ, if you are not spiritually prepared to die at this very moment then none of that matters. No amount of stuff, no amount of gear, no amount of ammo or food or water can ever take the place of the living water of Jesus Christ that He will give you – and it is this living water that sustains us - the Word of God and the precious Holy Spirit.

Christian prepping most likely is centered, for most believers, around End Time theology. In the last days the Bible indicates that Christians will be hated throughout all of the world for Jesus Christ namesake, it indicates also in the book of Daniel that our enemy will prevail against us physically until Christ returns and judgment is made in favor of His saints. In the book of Revelation of Jesus Christ we read also that Christians will be hunted down and martyred for their testimony of Our Lord Jesus Christ and the faith they hold near to heart.

So as you can read for the Christian there is much to prepare for, yet nothing we can do can stop what is written - for what is written will come to pass regardless. Embrace it, plan for it, and mitigate your families suffering if possible through God's grace.

To further clarify, the Bible indicates that there are three that make war against us as Christians in these last days - the Antichrist, the Beast, and the Dragon that old serpent of old.

It may seem overwhelming and a pointless endeavor to even consider prepping but God did not leave us alone – He gave His Holy Spirit to us, and In 1 John 4:4 We read the Greater is He that is in us then he that is in the World.

What an awesome God we serve, giving us mercy and grace when we sin and repent, giving us the wisdom and the awareness through His Word and through the Spirit of revelation to understand what's coming and to prepare for. He didn't leave us helpless by any means of the imagination. We each have the power and authority Christ has given us through His Holy Spirit – use it.

So how does the Christian prep or prepare for these things that must come to pass - Well for starters you have to be in excellent spiritual fitness. The Bible declares that in these last days that men's hearts would fail them for the fear of the knowledge of what is to come. We as Christian Preppers must learn to build up our courage and faith in Christ to proclaim boldly the Word of God - for it is the power of God unto Salvation. Knowing who you are in Christ and what your enemy's tactics are is the key – Understand Your authority in Christ!!

You know my question to you is this, if you had one opportunity, one last opportunity to speak to someone that you love before eternity came and took them away - what would you say? God has given us this very situation right now, in all honesty that's one of the reasons this book is being created, to reach out one last time before eternity is an ever present reality. This physical life has eternal consequences - one way or another after you die you will either go to heaven or you will go to hell, but there is no second chance once you're in eternity.

If you're a Prepper but not a Christian Prepper I would ask you one question – why are you prepping in the first place? Is it to save your life, your family's life, take back the country from out-of-control politicians? My assumption is that you are preparing because you wish to survive whatever scenario you see in the future or currently and if you have a family, I think I can say with relative confidence that you prepare so you can save their lives as well.

But understand this Mr. & Mrs. Prepper without Jesus Christ you fall short in your preps and your family, your love ones, your friends, and you will not survive. If you're serious about preparing then you must prepare in every aspect of one's life. Leaving out the most critical portion of your preparations is not intelligent and will surely leave you without hope, leave you without peace, and leave you without confidence.

Because without the Spirit of God dwelling in you, without Jesus Christ in your heart, you will not have that living water I spoke of earlier to refresh and center you – Jesus Christ is the well and without Him it's nothing but a desert.

Without Jesus Christ you will be driven mad by fear, uncertainty, and all the "What If's" that are in your mind. However, with Jesus Christ in your heart as your personal Lord and Savior you will have a peace, confidence, and boldness to do what must be done.

Now there's no way in a small little book like this that I can reach out to you the way that I truly want to and reason with you and encourage you to come to the knowledge of the truth in Christ Jesus before it is too late. If you think your gonna survive whatever may happen, whatever's going on – you may, but what if you don't?

Wouldn't you want to have the certainty of everlasting life for you and your family – this is a serious question and there is no way to express my heartfelt sincerity with mere words but I implore you as best I can in the love of God, and the love of Jesus Christ come to Him now because tomorrow is not guaranteed. I will leave some further insight at the end of this book if you are seriously considering opening your heart to Jesus Christ and getting right with God. I hope that you will check out the special gift in the back of the book to help guide you along the path to getting right with God.

If you do become a born-again Christian I want to hear from you - I want you to come to our website, is pretty easy to find, it's located in this book and throughout the web. I want you to drop me a line and reach out to me because I want to join with you in a real and personal way and help you mature in Christ through teaching you proper doctrine.

The door is always open I will never force anything on you but I will tell you straight, openly and honestly with the love of Christ the truth to the best of my ability. I hope you will take that step of faith and consider these words and truly join the family of God – I look forward to hearing from you soon.

"Spiritual Preparedness Always Comes Before Physical Preparedness that is the fundamental principle to remember about Christian Prepping" – AJF 03/21/2016 9:28pm

Chapter 2: Understand the Why

To understand the why is to understand all of prophecy. To understand the why is to be granted a Spirit of Revelation – for without the Spirit of Revelation no man can understand the why. For many Christians Preppers the why may be already innately within them from the Word of God and the Spirit of God bringing to remembrance those words.

What do we read in the Scriptures? We read about the Four Horsemen of the Apocalypse, we read about wars and rumors of wars, we read about famine and pestilence, earthquakes - we read about the beginning of sorrows in Matthew 24. In Matthew 24 it also talks about the fact that for Jesus Christ namesake, for our testimony, for our faith we will be hated in all of the world. My question to you the Christian Prepper is do you understand what happens after they hate us, after the label us, after they begin to discriminate against us and our faith?

If you're a brother or sister in Christ rightly dividing the Word of God you understand what comes next. They will set up and succeed at bringing in the Mark the Beast in Revelations 13:16, 17 - at which point the Christians will be backed into a corner in which they will not be able to buy or sell anything. Combine that with the fact that the entire world hates us and is discriminating against us – what is the logical and reasonable thing to do in such a situation - for certainly they will come, they will come in the night, they will come just like they came for Jesus in the night or the Jews, to round us up and to kill us. This is just what our enemy does.

But God in his mercy has given us the wisdom and the awareness to see the things that the world is blind to and to prepare accordingly. However, understand this - how the Christian prepares is massively different than how the average Prepper prepares.

So going back to the original question – why? The why is simple – God commands us to provide and to protect our families, He provides examples throughout the Old and New Testament of this very thing.

Whether it's an Ark, whether it's in the Lions Den, or whether it's during the tribulation God's always is in control and provides a way of escape for His people according to His will and the faith of His people.

Many people who call themselves Christians that believe in what they label a pre-tribulation rapture believe that God will supernaturally come back prior to any tribulation so they will not have to endure anything. However that is a false teaching, it is not Biblically sound – the same people most likely will be the ones in the great falling away.

God never said that He would rescue us from Tribulation; He said that we are not appointed to wrath. Jesus also spoke through Paul and indicated that we must endure hardship as a good soldier of Jesus Christ - what is hardship but tribulation.

The point here I'm trying to make is very simple to those that follow Christ, those that truly follow Christ they will have to endure the seals of God which is the tribulation but even through that God will provide for His people. Many of us will be martyred during this time in the 5th Seal, this is what's written, this is what must come to pass.

However at the same time I challenge believers out there, my brothers and sisters in Christ to consider the possibilities of preparing now to mitigate the amount of suffering that your family may have to endure. The Bible declares that God's people perish for lack of knowledge. So what does that mean to the Christian Prepper – it means that the more we are prepared both with knowledge and wisdom the more we stand a better chance not to parish for lacking it.

The choice of course is always yours whether to ignore warnings such as this and this book, warnings found in the Bible itself, or warnings deep within your spirit that are dropped there by the Holy Spirit – There're consequences for things that you do and their consequences for things that you do not do. I don't want to sound in such a way as to cause fear within your heart because the things that I speak and write to you today I speak in love encouraging you to get prepared and follow the examples that we have written ever so clearly in the Word of God.

My goal here is to put a sense of urgency within your heart and provide solutions as God enables through this book to deal systematically with helping you prepare to an adequate level in which you can fulfill the call of God on your life.

Verses to Consider to Be Prepared as the Lord directs us:

Luke: 22: 35-38: (35) And He said to them, "When I sent you without money bag, knapsack, and sandals, did you lack anything?" so they said, "Nothing." (36) Then He said to them, "But now, he who has a money bag, let him take it, and likewise a knapsack; and he who has no sword, let him sell his garment and buy one. (37) For I say to you that this which is written must still be accomplished in Me: 'And He was numbered with the transgressors. For the things concerning Me have an end." (38) So they said, "Lord, look, here are two swords." And He said to them, "It is enough."

Understanding God's Purpose and Plan During these Times

2 Timothy 2:3 - 3 You therefore must endure hardship as a good soldier of Jesus Christ.

Luke 21:12 But before all these things, they will lay their hands on you and persecute you, delivering you up to the synagogues and prisons. You will be brought before kings and rulers for My name's sake. (13) But it will turn out for you as an occasion for testimony. (14) Therefore settle it in your hearts not to meditate beforehand on what you will answer; (15) for I will give you a mouth and wisdom which all your adversaries will not be able to contradict or resist. (16) You will be betrayed even by parents and brothers, relatives and friends; and they will put some of you to death. (17) And you will be hated by all for My name's sake. (18) But not a hair of your head shall be lost. (19) By your patience possess your souls.

Chapter 3: Spiritual Survival

Understanding Spiritual Survival from a Christian perspective may be a little challenging at first glance. A sizable percentage of the prepping and survival community may consider themselves to be Christian; yet all too often, we talk about our survival plans as if God had nothing to do with them. Yet nothing could be farther from the truth. Without God's help and intervention, none of us have much of a chance of surviving anything – not even if we Bug Out.

Truly, we must be dependent upon God. But that dependence needs to start long before a disaster hits. If we expect to live by faith in the midst of a crisis and haven't been living by faith in our day-to-day lives, we are going to fail miserably. Learning to live by faith requires time and practice. It also requires going through the hard times, so that you can become accustomed to leaning on the Lord in the midst of them.

Any survival planning you do must include the Lord. That's where Spiritual Survival needs to start. You and I both need the guidance of the Holy Spirit to decide on everything from the right amount of gear, to the right place to Bug Out to. Trying to do these things in our own strength or knowledge puts us at a distinct disadvantage and in the same boat as those in the world; as if we didn't have God's help readily available to us.

There's more to Spiritual Survival than just asking God to help us make the right plans. To be honest, the average Christian today is spiritually lazy. We expect a pastor to do everything for us, rather than thinking for ourselves and doing what God calls us to do ourselves. But what are we going to do when that pastor isn't there? Have you made plans to bring your pastor along as part of your Spiritual Survival plan? Do you have enough supplies to feed him and his family too?

One of the beauties of the New Testament is the priesthood of the believer. We don't need a pastor or priest between God, and ourselves because we already have one in Jesus Christ.

Jesus, in His role as the High Priest, intercedes for us continually before the Father. So, while a pastor maybe useful (If they're not working as part of the clergy response teams), they are not a requirement for us to find and depend on God.

However, few believers are truly prepared to encounter God on their own. We are a nation of spiritual babies, expecting our pastors to change our diapers and give us our bottles. That won't get us through a survival situation and enable Spiritual Survival. We're going to have to know the Word of God to understand how to stand on our own two feet, as well as how to pastor others.

When a disaster or significant persecution arises, we're going to have to be ready to spiritually care for our families. The Bible you bring will be the only "pastor" you have. And if you lose your Bible – You're going to need to know the Bible; know how to teach it and know how to live it. We're also going to have to know how to give counsel from it; pray for our families when they are sick and witness to those we encounter. Discipleship is the Great Commission but it starts in our own home first.

You will need to be prepared to feed your family spiritually, so that their faith can remain steadfast and strong. Regular family Bible studies or even home church services will need to become part of your Spiritual Survival plan. If you've never experienced God in the middle of a meadow in the mountains, you're missing out. Some of the greatest spiritual experiences of your life may very well happen after you Bug Out and are dependent on God.

To do that, we need to prepare ourselves today; otherwise, we won't be ready for the life we are going to live tomorrow. If you are not a serious student of the Word of God, then I've got to say that you aren't ready right now. You're still expecting someone else to do it for you; and as long as you're doing that, you're not going to know how to count on God, when things go bad.

Chapter 4: What is God's Plan

If you still reading here in chapter 4 I commend your dedication as most people pick up a book and never get past the second chapter, for that alone I commend your dedication. Let's now discuss God's plan for these dark times. There are countless examples throughout history and throughout the Bible of God commanding his people to bug out. I won't go too much in depth or give too many examples in this particular section if you would like more in-depth look at bugging out from a biblical perspective I encourage you to read our book Biblical Bug Out: Don't Bug In - Follow The Calling. Yes that is a selfish plug for our book but I do feel that this book can help fast-track anyone who is a believer in Jesus Christ get a firm understanding of bugging out and why it's so critical to plan for that. Nevertheless let us continue. Escape and Evasion, this is a military term that has to do with eluding one's enemy during a military conflict. This is the very principle God has directed us to use during these dark times.

Let's examine a Scripture verse:

God says flee to the mountains and don't go back to get anything – therefore, watch and pray and be ready at all times – Matt. 24:15-20 / Mark 13

Mark 13: 14 -19 [14 "So when you see the 'abomination of desolation, spoken of by Daniel the prophet, standing where it ought not" (let the reader understand), "then let those who are in Judea flee to the mountains. (15) Let him who is on the housetop not go down into the house, nor enter to take anything out of his house. (16) And let him who is in the field not go back to get his clothes. (17) But woe to those who are pregnant and to those who are nursing babies in those days! (18) And pray that your flight may not be in winter. (19) For in those days there will be tribulation, such as has not been since the beginning of the creation which God created until this time, nor ever shall be.]

Now the abomination of desolation spoken of by the prophet Daniel what does this truly mean. If you read the King James Version that uses the terminology "It".

I propose a question at this time, has the abomination of desolation already taken place? A third temple has been rebuilt - "it" stands in Brazil. Any Christian or even any Jew for that matter understands that Solomon's Temple is not supposed to be in Brazil.

This is debatable of course and they're many that would say this or that but one thing is for certain a third Temple has been built. That fact alone should give cause to many to evaluate and research if the abomination of desolation has already taken place or may be about to happen.

This third Temple was built to exact specifications of the original one with material imported from Israel and the Middle East. A quick search online will reveal all the information one would need.

I've heard rumors for years about secret plans that the Jews in Israel have for rebuilding a third Temple I'm not sure of the accuracy of these reports but as I mentioned a third Temple has already been built and it stands in Brazil.

Chapter 5: Educating Yourself

Educating yourself is like investing in yourself and your family for the future. The more that you educate yourself on things like being prepared, survival, and spiritual warfare the better off you and your family will be. Nowadays college students can spend anywhere from $30,000.00 to $150,000.00 for a college education - whether it's a lawyer, teacher, or doctor Though these professions may have certain values to them, if you were any one of those people in those particular professions in the middle of the woods or middle of the forest would you be able to survive?

If your profession that you spent thousands of dollars educating yourself on is pointless when it comes to actual physical survival skills you need to educate yourself now.

If you were willing to spend thousands of dollars on a college education that honestly isn't worth that much nowadays and will not prepare you or your family to survive in the middle of nowhere you got to ask yourself what is the point. Now what would happen if you invested the same amount of money you spent to go to college on being prepared?

I believe that the Native American Indians had it right - everyone was trained in particular skills that enabled them to live off of the land in a harmonious type of way without destroying it but living in balance. If you spent thousands of dollars on a skill, on a trade, or on a degree and you don't have the skills necessary still to survive off the land it's time to reinvest in educating yourself and gain these viable lifesaving skills.

Now thankfully God in His mercy and grace has enabled you to learn through books like this whether online or physically. Additionally with the advent of the Internet and companies like You Tube there is a tremendous amount of resources available free of charge or with books like this at a minimum cost. The amount of value that you can get from one awesome book or one great video that can literally give you the skills to save you or your family member's life – how can you honestly put a price tag on that? It's like asking how much is your life worth, how much is your family's life worth – thankfully most of these skills can be picked up by investing more time than money.

I would encourage every brother and sister out there to get a small collection of books that they're actually going to read as well as some small manuals with specific detailed information that you put in your bug out bag just in case you forget a particular skill to have the book as a resource. In fact I would say every bug out bag should probably have two books at least in them, a King James Version Bible and a survival manual.

In addition to small group of books I would also encourage you to create a You Tube account and learn how to develop play list. Then start adding videos to your playlist that teach you solid information on key areas like shelter building, water purification, fire building, knife selection, etc.

All of this education is great but much like your gear if you don't test it out prior to needing it you're not going to know if it works and you may be up that proverbial river without a paddle. It's absolutely critical to get out on whatever land you plan to survive on and test the skills that you have acquired through reading and observing – it's what we call "Dirt Time".

After reading and observing the next logical step is doing, practicing the knowledge that you have learned. Thus after practicing that knowledge turns into wisdom and that wisdom turns into practical application of learned skills. The American Christian Defense Alliance, Inc. outdoor ministry of the Burning Bush Survival and Preparedness School is currently also in the development of various courses to help prepare you. Please visit our website and sign up for a mailing list for future updates.

Chapter 6:
Five Foundations of Survival

Selecting a Survival Knife

Of all your survival equipment, the single most important piece (besides your Bible) is a good knife. Many experts have agreed that if they had to pick only one piece of equipment to use, it would be their knife. That makes sense really, as you can make much of the rest of what you need out of what nature provides you, if you have a knife to work with. No other single piece of equipment does more.

The question then becomes, what sort of knife should you buy? There are a plethora of knives available on the market, available for a wide range of prices and with a large range of options to choose from. There are even knives marketed as survival knives, which contain all sorts of extra equipment to help you survive. So, what's the best?

First of all, this is one place where quality counts more than anything else. If you are going to depend on a knife to help you survive, you need one that is going to hold up under the strain of heavy use, without a risk of it breaking and hopefully with the ability to maintain a good, sharp edge.

With that being our criteria, the first thing to consider is the knife's construction. You want a fixed-blade knife, rather than a folding one. Folding knives can break more easily and the lock can slip at an inopportune moment, causing a serious injury. A folding knife is fine as a backup, but your primary knife should be fixed-blade.

The blade needs to have a full tang. This refers to the part of the blade that extends back through the handle. Manufacturers of cheap knives use partial tangs to save money. But the handle is likely to break right at the end of the tang, when the knife is subject to extreme pressure, leaving you with a blade that doesn't have a handle. That's awfully hard to work with.

I would recommend a blade style that gives you a strong point, as the point is the most fragile part of the blade. Drop point knives are pretty good for this, as well as tonto blades. I personally like clip point knives a lot, because you get a sharper point; but those are not as good for survival knives. The same can be said for dagger point knives. Besides, you don't need a fighting knife as a survival knife, you need a working tool.

The other main issue is the steel that the knife is made of. Most commercially made knives today are made of some sort of stainless steel. That is nice in that it doesn't rust, but stainless steel doesn't hold an edge like high-carbon steel does. The best knives have been made of high-carbon steel for centuries.

Some of the best high-carbon steel comes out of Solingen, Germany. This town is known for their knives, most of which are kitchen knives. However, there are a few companies in Solingen who produce outdoor knives. Just make sure you're actually getting one made in Solingen, and not a cheap knock-off.

Another very popular option is true Damascus steel. This is actually a layered laminate of high-carbon steel and a softer spring steel. The two together provide an excellent edge, while keeping the knife from becoming brittle. High-carbon steel by itself is so hard, that it can be brittle at times. Damascus steel is the one truly obvious steel option, because its layers cause a striped pattern in the knife's blade.

But other than Damascus steel, it's very hard to tell the difference between other types of steel. Not all manufacturers will give you that information, essentially expecting you to trust them for the selection of a good steel for your knife.

There are a number of companies who produce excellent knives. It seems that each survival expert has their favorite. ESSE, Tops, Cold Steel, and Becker are popular brands, all three of which specialize in survival and combat knives. The old standbys of K-Bar and Gerber are good choices as well; especially for people who don't want to spend as much money.

Whatever brand you ultimately choose, realize that you're not going to get a quality knife at a bargain basement price. Cheap knives are just that... cheap. Most especially, they use cheap steel, which won't hold an edge. To get a good knife, you're going to have to spend some money; somewhere between $70 and $200.

Avoid knives with a built-in saw blade, unless the saw blade is on the back side of the knife. A two inch long saw blade isn't going to accomplish much for you and it's going to shorten the knife's effective blade, reducing what you can do with it. You should also avoid "gimmick" knives, which are selling you a survival kit in a knife. Remember, to give you the other stuff, they have to reduce the cost of the knife. That's done by using cheaper steel.

Shelter

Regardless of whether you're trying to make your way home after a disaster, trying to bug out after a disaster, or just trying to make your way out after being lost in the wilderness, shelter is going to be an important factor.

Shelter is one of the things we use to protect ourselves from the weather and maintain our body heat, making it one of our most important survival priorities.

The biggest killer in the wild is hypothermia, the loss of body heat. This can happen year-round, as the ambient air temperature is normally lower than our body's temperature. When we get wet, either through excessive sweating, rain or from falling in a body of water, our bodies shed heat rapidly. Without shelter, it doesn't take long for hypothermia to set in.

That's why it's important to always carry some sort of shelter materials in your bug out bag or EDC bag (everyday carry bag). It doesn't take much; you don't need an expensive backpacking tent. A simple tarp and some cordage will help you make a decent shelter in a pinch.

But more important than the materials you are carrying is to start with what nature offers. There are a lot of things that can be used for shelter, when in the wild. Some can be used as they are, while others may need to be improved with the help of your tarp and cordage. Either way, starting with what nature provides makes the job easier.

So, what sorts of things can you look for in nature to use as shelter? Caves – Check to make sure they are unoccupied, before going in. Rock Outcroppings – They will often have places where two or three rocks have a space between them which can quickly be converted to a cave. Undercut Embankments – Rivers or flash floods can undercut an embankment, creating a wide but shallow cave. With a wind screen in front and a fire in-between, this makes a comfortable shelter.

Overturned Trees – The space below the tree can be cleaned out for a shelter or the root mass makes a good back wall for a shelter. Thickets of Trees – Often saplings will grow close enough together to create a hidden spot which blocks off the wind.

You might have to cut a few saplings out of the middle and string your tarp overhead, but it will provide a great windbreak. Other than the caves, you'll have to make some modifications in pretty much all these cases.

That's where your tarp and cordage come in. The tarp can either be used as a roof or as walls, depending on the needs of your particular shelter.

Another great material that you can find in the wild is to use tree branches. Layered against the side of the shelter or on the roof, they shed rain well and provide good resistance to break up the wind.

The key here, more than anything, is being able to improvise. Simply opening your eyes and seeing what nature has already created is the first step in creating any shelter. Then, it's just a matter of figuring out how to make that shelter more rain and wind proof, as well as where you can place your fire to keep you warm.

Fire

Fire has to be one of the most useful tools that God has given mankind. While our main use of fire is to help keep us warm, it goes beyond that in meeting our needs. Fire also provides us with light, a means of cooking our food and even a way of purifying water. All this makes fire an essential for survival. While we could theoretically survive without it, trying to do so requires much more effort than building and maintaining the fire does. So, it ultimately makes more sense to have a fire as a part of any survival effort, than not to have it. Actually, it's one of the first things we should do.

If you've ever watched someone try to start a fire, who doesn't know what they're doing, you should have a pretty good appreciation of the difficulty involved. If we were to analyze the fire starting methodology of these people, we'd probably quickly encounter that they are causing much of their own problem.

Most specifically, they aren't working their way up through the different types of flammable materials correctly.

What do I mean by that? I mean starting with tinder, working your way up to kindling and then to the fuel for your fire. Most of the time, they try to jump from tinder to fuel or sometimes from a match to fuel. What's the difference between these things? Tinder consists of things that will catch fire easily from one match or other fire starter. You can include dry grass, newspaper, char-cloth, dryer lint and dry moss in this category. Every fire needs tinder to get it started. Kindling is small flammable material that will burn longer than the rapid-burning tinder and allow the flame to grow so that it will ultimately catch the fuel on fire. Usually, we're talking about sticks the diameter of your finger here. Larger sticks can be used, if they are made into a "fuzz stick."

Fuel is what your fire is going to burn to provide you with heat. Typically, we're talking about pieces about the diameter of your arm. This gives a nice balance between catching fire fairly easily and not burning too quickly. About the only time you want chunks of wood larger than this, is if you are setting the fire up to burn through the night.

These three types of material need to be set up in a teepee or pyramid structure, so that the burning tinder can catch the kindling on fire and then the kindling can catch the fuel on fire. As flame, like any other heat rises, this is typically done by putting the tinder on the bottom, with the kindling above it and the fuel forming the outer shell.

There are many ways you can provide an initial spark, ember or flame to the fuel, in order to start a fire. Survival instructors collect fire starting methods like some people collect baseball cards. But if you have simple fire starters, you might want to use them. This usually means waterproof matches or a butane lighter.

A lighter is probably the best single fire starter you can carry. A typical lighter will start about 1,000 fires, if it is used carefully and not wasted. It's compact, fairly water resistant and reliable. The only problem is that it won't work in cold weather. But to solve this problem, you can keep the lighter inside your clothing to keep it warm.

Most survival instructors say you should carry two primary and two secondary forms of fire starting. Lighters and matches are the primary means. Things like metal matches, Ferro Rods, magnifying glasses, 0000 steel wool and a battery, and a bow drill all fall into the category. Other than for practice, you really only want to use one of these secondary methods in the case where you don't have your primary methods. I prefer to carry two lighters, one of which is totally waterproof, rather than mess with those other methods (although I have them too).

One other thing you should always carry for starting a fire is an accelerant. This is something, usually chemical, which will burn readily.

While the term "accelerant" is normally used in association with arson, it's the correct term to use in this case as well. If you do a search online for "fire starters" you'll find some of these, along with things like the Metal Match and Ferro Rod. Some of the best are cube shaped and individually wrapped.

A fire accelerant is especially useful when it is wet out. You really don't want to use them all the time, but if it is raining, you'll be glad you have one. You can make your own as well, by working petroleum jelly into cotton balls. One cotton ball, treated in this way, will burn for over three minutes, making it great for getting a stubborn fire started.

Water

Water is one of the key elements to life and survival. During a crisis situation, SHTF, or your Bug Out finding and making potable water is a must. It's important to understand the time frame that your body has for needing water. Your body runs best when properly hydrated each and every day. Lack of hydration will cause lack of focus and lack of focus will cause poor decisions to be made – it's not just physical thing - your body needing water.

Water affects everything. Your body can only survive approximately 3 days without water. That being said it's vital to understand how to find water and how to make it drinkable.

There lots of filters and purifiers on the market today each one having its own unique benefits and disadvantages. Check our website for current recommendations. However, having a steel container to boil water in will go a long way to making water potable.

Now considering that the mentality and the plan that God has for us is to escape and evade we might not be in a position in which fire would be such a good idea. There are lots of ways to hide a fire such as a Dakota fire pit but in all reality sometimes it's better not to take the chance and build a fire while being hunted. You have to remember, even if they can't see your fire they might be able to smell your smoke or see a smoke signal. If you built a fire close to the thick evergreen tree you might be able to hide the smoke for those around but it's still not a good idea while in escape and evade mode.

Therefore, that's when certain water filters water purifiers come in the play. They enable you to have fresh clean drinking potable water without the need of the fire – a significant tactical advantage for you while on the run. Again check our website for the most updated list of recommendations.

When trying to acquire up in the Surrey water for survival as you bug out there a few options. You could attempt to catch water with a tarp or poncho and drain that water into a steel container and boil it. The fire is not an option that you could still drain the water into your container; however, this is where you would need something similar to a Life Straw (which is a lightweight filter that you drink out of).

Another option for the Christian Prepper would be to read the terrain to determine if there is a stream, Creek or other potential body of water in the local vicinity. Obviously all water flows downhill so as you continue to move down there is a greater chance to find water.

This is where being prepared and having foresight comes into play. If you have prepared your bug out bag appropriately prior to needing it you should have your water containers already filled as well as the appropriate necessities to process water appropriately for safe consumption.

Another great option is water tabs. Now for those with a thyroid condition you may want to watch your iodine consumption. However, these are a great option as they are the latest option available and can be thrown into any pocket or kit. Just remember you're still good and need a steel container I cannot over emphasize the importance of the steel container. I should also mention that it's important to have a wide mouth steel container, as this will give you more options and make your life just a little bit easier on the go.

Food

Everything has it's purpose in your systems and Long Term Food Storage is no different. That being said, I would also say that All LTFS is only a backup to other backups you have in place.

You should strive to live a life in which you produce your own food or source it directly from nature - Don't rely on others to feed you, chances are you will no doubt starve at a rapid rate.

Long Term Food Storage should not be confused with food that you utilize in your Bug Out Bag / Go Bag or Bug Out Vehicle or in a Cache'. This is not the intended purpose for LTFS.

For these systems you should consider MREs (Meals Ready to Eat) and Mainstay Food Ration Bars (3600 Cal.). Both also make great additions to any cache and do not require any water to actually cook or produce ... Unlike the Long Term Food Storage options which will require water to make.

Grab & Go should be just that to limit the amount of extra worry in your food preparations. Furthermore, take time to explore, study, and learn about wild edibles - this knowledge alone could save your life.

Grab & Go Options (No Preparation Needed) - Self life of 5-7 Years

MREs (Meals Ready-to-Eat)
Mainstay Food Rations (3600 Cal)

LTFS = Long Term Food Storage

There are a lot of options out there for anyone when it comes to Long Term Food Storage (LTFS) including Do It Yourself Options such as canning or vacuum sealing your own food. If your resources and abilities permit it this is the cheapest option to get the most bang for your buck. Yet when you need to Bug Out all that food stays right there unless you have it cached in a safe location. LTFS Companies that offer who have freeze dried food in buckets help with the transportation or transition of such food but it still is in a bucket so you can't bring it when you go on foot.

Now I've done the math here and for some of the LTFS options or plans if you would you could purchase Grab & Go Back Packing Options such as Backpackers Pantry. I recently did just that.

One thing that really gets to me is how the so called LTFS business doesn't include any real meat in their meals - What do you see out there? Pasta, Soups, Rice, Some Beans, and a whole lot of Cheese. I'm not sure about anyone else but I keep thinking of the old Wendy's commercial when they say, "Where the Beef"

99% of the time you have to purchase the meat separately and it's ridiculous in price, so what's another way to move forward with a practical plan that gives you the protein you will need in a stressful situation? Backpackers Pantry or another similar option – and with these when you Bug Out they come with you, well at least some of it – Try that will a 50lbs of Rice, good luck, lol. Also go as organic and healthy as possible - if you put "Crap" in your body you literally will get "Crap" out.

Can goods are another great way to get protein on the cheap, relatively speaking that is. Check out your local wholesale club - We shop at BJs and they are doing a great job moving to more organic items. However, again just remember you're not going to throw a bunch of can goods in your Bug Out Bag, it's just too heavy.

Now I don't want you to walk away thinking that long-term food storage is a waste of time, it's not. You don't know what situations can take place and for that reason alone you should have long-term food storage. The Word of God says no one knows the day or the hour but we are able to read the seasons – that being said is good to plan accordingly. Remember there will be famine throughout the land prior, I repeat prior to us being hated and persecuted and martyred. So to help us endure and whether the storm it's critical to have enough food stored up both at your house and other various locations.

How much food? Well that honestly depends on the size of your family, on how long you desire to feed them - six months, a year, or maybe five years. As a Christian Prepper I would recommend at least four years' worth of food to be stored up if at all financially possible. I would recommend freeze-dried as the best option. Freeze-dried food does carry a higher price point but you are receiving all the nutrients unlike the dehydrated foods.

Long Term Food Storage does have its place in the Christian Preppers life especially if you have a Bug Out Retreat or if you don't plan to Bug Out. For the Christian Prepper who has the resources it would be a great idea to purchase LTFS and Cache it in various places. Keep in mind with any LTFS Company you have to Read the Fine Print and know what to look for. There is an Art and a Science to buying LTFS. Our organization does support some LTFS as an option and is partnering with selected companies that provide the greatest value and benefits to those we serve.

Check our website for the latest reviews on companies and their products.

Your stockpile of food for you and your family should consist of a multi layered system where options such as bugging out and bugging in are considered. Additionally, caches of preparations and food along commonly travel routes and approximately 5 miles away from your home should be considered as vital links in your overall survival plan.

Chapter 7: How to Start Prepping

Developing Your Systems & Planning
Things Out - Including SOPs

First and foremost you need to understand what the Word of God has to say about preparing, as well as prophecy in these last days. From there it will be important to start to understand how to prepare by reading books like this. After learning how to get things organized and having a basic operational framework for your preparedness objectives learning and practicing survival skills is next up on the to do list.

The following are some considerations to think about to help you develop your systems and SOPs (Standard Operating Procedures) for you and your family. Every Family will have slightly different needs so there was no point in attempting to add a universal plan – something like that does not exist and if it did would most likely have very little real world application for you and your family.

Family Preparedness Plans: Family Rules of Preparedness – Develop Habits to Keep You Alive

Having a clearly understandable Threat Level System is important to understand the risk level you and your family face at a given moment in time. This system should give a basic understanding of the situation so you and your family can be on the same page without the need for too much conversation.

There's an old saying, "Lose Lips Sink Ships" – not sure who said that but the saying is very accurate. Saying too much in today's world with electronic surveillance techniques reaching ever increasing capabilities and government's out of control invasion into our lives poses a significant security threat to those being falsely labeled as a threat or worse yet – labeled for extermination. Remember your advisory the devil walks around like a roaring lion seeking whom he may devour.

The Word of God is clear how we should handle the devil – Resist the devil and he must flee! Many of us as Christians may think the need for such as system is not necessary but what if I told you right now by doing a simply search online you can find US Government documents labeling Christians as a "Domestic Terrorist Threat". In fact Christians who are attempting to stand for truth like Pastor Chuck Baldwin or Ron Paul were put on such a list and labeled while running for President of the United States in 2008. Thereafter in 2012, we saw the IRS begin to target Christian businesses (including churches) that had or were seeking tax-exempt status – coincidence or conspiracy?

As absurd as this may sound to the uninformed Christian it is nevertheless a reality that we must face head on to have any hope of preparing properly. I encourage you to do the research for yourself, start with the MIAC Report and Project Megiddo and see just how far the rabbit hole goes.

Throughout history we see the same patterns prior to Democide, Genocide, or as some would call it a Holocaust.

I would encourage every believer to check out the Voice of the Martyrs website and other sites to see how much the average Christian is being persecuted throughout the world, some I would even consider a silent holocaust as the mainstream media deliberately ignores their suffering. Very soon this will turn into a "hot war" on the Christian believer and thus the reasons for the Threat Level System as well as all our plans.

Here is a basic system and things to consider and plan for:

Threat Level System & Codes

- Green
- Amber
- Yellow
- Orange
- Red

- People involved in our network and their contact information
- Communications (How to Contact each other during an Emergency)
- Meet Up Locations
- Routes to Bug Out Locations
- Alternative Routes Home from Work
- Methods of Travel if Roads are closed (Include Maps)
- Cache Locations (with Contents Listed & Maps to them)
- Specific Assigned Roles & Duties During Emergencies
- Vital Records (Copies of Important documents, Insurance, birth records, SS Cards,
- Immigration status, Health Records, etc)
- Bug Out Bag / Go Bag
- Bug Out Vehicle
- Bug Out Information
- Mountain Retreat / Bug Out Location Information
- Bug In Information

Tactical Considerations

Tactical Considerations for the Christian who is attempting to survive a hostile situation, possibly with their family, is one of the major considerations to think about. The greatest single danger posed in any survival situation is that posed by the two-legged predators that you and I will face. As unprepared people become hungry, they will also become desperate. This will cause some to turn to criminal means to get what they need for themselves and their families.

This poses a bit of a quandary for the Christian. On one hand, we have a responsibility to provide for and protect our families. But on the other hand, we have a responsibility to feed the poor. Only in this case, feeding the poor might mean taking the food out of our own children's mouths to feed total strangers. Maybe they'll still eat today, but with limited supplies, feeding others may mean that we run out of supplies for our own family.

We are also faced with the risk of these predators attacking our families. They aren't going to listen to reason and they aren't going to be easily turned away. If we have the supplies they need, they will attack time and again, until they gain the victory.

The Bible tells us in Deuteronomy that killing in defense of home and family is acceptable. This is where the legal principle known as the "castle doctrine" came from. As long as we are killing in defense, we are okay. It is only when we attack others for personal gain, that we break God's Law. The American Christian Defense Alliance, Inc. very name indicates our defensive posture that falls in line with this Biblical principle.

So, what do we do? There are two parts of preparing ourselves in this regard. The first is making our home more defendable, by "hardening the exterior. This simply means making it harder to break into. The second part is acquiring firearms and becoming proficient in their use. Simply owning firearms isn't enough; we must learn and practice, until we reach the point where we can make Wyatt Earp himself proud.

Hardening your home means more than just putting a deadbolt on your door and locking your windows. Any criminal can kick open a dead bolted door, and glass windows are easy to break. You're going to have to go beyond the conventional wisdom if you want to keep your home safe in a time of emergency.

The weak point on your door is the door frame. So, replace the normal striker plate on the door with a security striker plate. This is a bigger striker plate, so that the force of any kick will be spread over a larger area.

When you install it, use 3" screws, so that you are attaching it through the door frame and into the studs behind. That will force them to break a whole lot more than just the door frame to get the door open.

While you're at it, replace the short screws in the door's hinges with the same long screws, strengthening that side of the door as well. Replacing the standard hinges with security hinges is a good idea too, as the security hinges act somewhat like a small deadbolt, securing the hinge side of the door too.

Windows are hard to secure, but there are two options. The first is security window film. This self-adhesive film is installed on the inside of the window. It acts much like the inner layer on a windshield, preventing it from coming apart, even when broken. While it can still be broken out, that requires breaking out all the glass in the window. The other option is to put burglar bars over the windows. Custom burglar bars are better than the universal ones.

Once installed, the bad guys would have to use a truck and a chain to pull them off your home and gain access – Yet another tactical consideration.

All of these tactical considerations to harden your home only delay the bad guys. Ultimately, it's up to you and your guns to protect your family. But keeping them out gives you time to react, grabbing your guns and taking a stand to fight them off.

However, tactical considerations for the Christian looking to survive a hostile situation (one in which we will be hated in all the world for Christ's name sake) should not focus so much on tactical considerations in a stationary position like your home. We must focus more on tactical considerations when Bugging Out. For more information on tactical considerations when Bugging Out please see the American Christian Defense Alliance, Inc. Book: Biblical Bug Out: Don't Bug In – Follow The Calling

Considerations for your Wife & Children

No one likes thinking about disasters and emergency situations, but the simple truth is that we are all vulnerable to them. Each year, hundreds, if not thousands of people, are affected by various natural disasters and the key to survival is preparedness.

It is especially important for women to be prepared for emergency situations. Having an emergency plan can help you remain calm, despite the circumstances, and help others that might be in need.

Women, in particular tend to be more anxious than men, which might provoke a sense of panic in case of a disaster. In the same time, women are drawn to people in need, and the key to helping those around you is preparing in advance.

The best way to prepare for a disaster is to know the proper way to respond to a variety of emergency situations. Knowing what and where the available community resources are is a great place to start – it will provide you with a sense of security, while helping you map out an emergency plan. It's often the first responders to a disaster that make the most difference, and, as a woman and wife, you are responsible not only for yourself, but for everyone around you – including spouses and children. Having an emergency kit around at all times is one of the best ways to be prepared for any sort of disaster. It should include crucial items that will aid survival, such as blankets, radio, hygiene items, as well as at least three-day supply of food and water for everyone.

Being prepared is important not only for women, but for all people. Knowing that you have an emergency plan will help you remain calm, in case there's an emergency situation, and will provide you with the opportunity to help the people around you, and make sure your loved ones are safe and protected.

Communications

Ham Radio is the most reliable form of communication for the Christian Prepper there is – Period. After extensive research I believe that the Ham Radio is simply the best form of communication for anyone truly concerned with getting through to their love ones in an emergency situation. Ham Radio gives you so many options that other forms of communication simply can't. Furthermore, Ham Radios give you outstanding range and clarity for slightly more than other radios.

Personally I wanted to go with a hand held ham radio that I could carry with me at all times, or throw it in my Bug Out Bag and be good to go. I have also invested in mobile unit for my wife and me. Both Kenwood and Yaesu put out great ham radios. We have Kenwood mobile units and Yaesu hand held units.

Now keep in mind that it is advantageous to pre-program you radios and their frequencies so you and your wife don't give out the frequency you going to - all you need to do is say go to channel 7 or whatever channel you are going to.

One thing I would caution is not to purchase a Ham Radio with a built in GPS unit. This technology while convenient today could spell disaster for you tomorrow. Having other forms of communications is a plus, but they all have their respective limitations.

Cellphones: The best cellphone to have in the event of an emergency would be from Sprint or Nextel. The phones that have the direct connect feature and are ideal in a crisis situation, as they are able to operate without the cell towers as two way radios for up to approximately 6 miles. So for an everyday carry to replace your current phone – not bad. You can add a fixed antenna to some of their phones which also increases their range. For more information check out the Sprint website.

However, If you looking for privacy and security overall the older Blackberry phones are a great choice. Some

"Private" cell networks actually convert these phones even more to enhance the privacy feature already build in.
Now, yes you did just read it correctly - there are private cellphone networks - if your interested in your privacy check them out.

Now for the average person that is not tech savvy there are a few options. Some options include the following:

- CB Radios:
- FRS/GRMS
- Garmin 530:
- Satellite Phones:

CB Radios have 40 channels and is what most "Truckers" use to check out traffic and such. These are also popular for people who are into four wheeling or off road driving as well as families who enjoy camping.

They are pretty straight forward to use and curtain channels are monitored by the police in the event of an emergency such as channel 9. While channel 9 is typically reserved for emergency calls channel 19 is liken to a chat room and is the channel of choice for the over the road Truckers.

Unfortunately they have only a limited range of approximately 4 miles. Additionally the communication is on the AM frequency which means the audio quality is not always the greatest. These radios do not require any special license to operate but are good for a backup nothing more.

FRS and GRMS Radios are normally sold as one radio despite being two separate bands.
FRS stands for Family Radio Service. No license is required to own or operate these here in the United States and offers great voice quality. The FRS radios operate on UHF or Ultra High Frequency and are part of the FM Band.

Unfortunately the draw back on these radios is the face that they have limited range. If you read on a package 20, 30, or 45 miles of operation do not believe it. You can find these in most outdoor stores or even at most electronic departments in major retailers. For the average citizen these radios have effectively replaced the old CBs or Citizen Band Radios. As a result of their overall quality and inexpensive price point many small business use these radios. Again consider these only has a backup and for no more than a mile or two away.

GRMS is short for General Mobile Radio Service. These radios are very similar to the FRS radios in just about every way but do require an FCC license to operate. The way this license works in the United States is that you complete the application and pay the fee, then you and your entire family are covered under the license.

The enforcement of not completing the paperwork in unknown but if you're going to operate on these channels just fill out the paperwork to cover yourself. If you're going to purchase an FRS type radio I would recommend the Garmin walkie talkie style GPS handhelds like the 530 model.

One of the coolest things, well at least for me is the idea that I can be anywhere in the world and talk to someone I love. Satellite phones enable you to do just that. They are expense in every since of the word but if you do have the money this might be the best option for you. As there is little of a learning curve and you don't need any special license - but man oh man is it expensive. That's why for the average Christian Prepper I say Ham Radio is simply the best option, especially when bugging out.

Navigation

In today's modern world, GPS navigation has taken over from pretty much all other ways we used to navigate. But what will happen when those satellites go down? An EMP would easily take them down, rendering most of us unable to find our way much farther than back and forth to work.

It doesn't even take something as serious as an EMP to shut down our navigation. People's batteries go out all the time, leaving them without a way of using their phone and its installed GPS. While that isn't a problem if we're going back and forth to places we frequent, it can become a big problem if we have to go someplace different. It can be an even bigger problem if we're lost or a disaster has blocked our normal route.

Generally speaking, navigation requires a map and compass. The map gives you a pictorial representation of the ground you are passing over and the compass shows you which direction you're going.

Assuming you can find where you are on the map, and you know which direction you're going, you should be able to find pretty much anything.

Of course, that means having a map that's appropriate for what you're doing. A common street map isn't going to help you, unless you're driving on the streets. That's typically the easiest sort of navigation, as the street signs help you to find where you are on the map.

However, once you get away from the streets, you need a topographical map. You can get these for the entire country through the U.S. Geological Survey's website. Topographical maps differ in that while they do show us streets, they are more focused on showing us the shape of the land. Their main feature is a series of squiggly brown lines, which are referred to as contour lines. These show the height above sea level for anything on the map. You can tell hills and mountain peaks, because they will be shown on the map as a series of concentric rings, even if they are lopsided ones.

Those become your main landmarks for navigation in most circumstances.

If you can identify two or more terrain features (such as those mountain peaks) on your map, you can locate yourself. All you need to do is to point your compass at that peak and see what the direction, measured in degrees, is from you to it. The direction from it to you will then be that direction plus or minus 180 degrees; this is called a reciprocal bearing.

With two or more reciprocal bearings, you can draw lines (lightly, in pencil, so they can be erased) from the mountain peaks. Where those lines intersect is where you are.

To walk from where you are to where you are going you simply need to plan out your route on the map and break it down into directions that your compass can help you identify. Let's say you are going to follow a curving valley. The first direction you need to go is straight east, or 90 degrees.

Then, you'll need to turn 30 degrees north to follow the valley. Okay, so you set 0 degrees directly under the needle on your compass. Then, you look for 90 degrees. That's the direction you need to go. Find a landmark in that direction and start walking towards it.

But what do you do if you don't even have a map and compass? That's where you have to rely on landmarks to help you navigate. In the Old West days, people traveled back and forth across the country, simply by following landmarks. Cowboys would sit around the campfire, describing places they've been and the landmarks to use in order to find those places. Each became a walking encyclopedia of directions to get to different places.

One trick they used, which is very valuable for us, is that of going downhill. If you're lost in the wilderness, start walking downhill. That does two things for you. First of all, it will help you find water, as water always flows downhill.

Secondly, it will help you find civilization, as people tend to build roads and cities in the flatlands. As you work your way downhill, you can be assured that you are getting closer to civilization.

Fire Arms & Weapons

Firearms, one of the most controversial subjects here in America yet number two in the original Bill of Rights. The American Christian Defense Alliance, Inc. believes very strongly in the right of the people to keep and bare arms to protect themselves and their love ones. The American Christian Defense Alliance, Inc. believes that firearms of any kind are merely a tool to ensure that liberty is past down to future generations and rejects the statement that, "Guns Kill People" in full. Firearms can do nothing in and of themselves, it is the person behind the operation of the firearm that is fully responsible for any and all actions in which may cause injury of some kind.

Remember this: every time a nation has enacted a law to make firearms illegal great tyranny has risen up ... From Nazi Germany, to Communist Russia all dictators would agree gun control works. When gun control works massive amounts of people are murdered by the state. Professor John Lott has two good books about gun ownership and crime. Both of his books indicate that where there is more gun control there is more crime.

Don't let it happen again here in America. I urge all of you reading this to get prepared ASAP because the time is coming and now is when this nation will seek to take away our 2nd Amendment Right to keep and bare arms. We here at the American Christian Defense Alliance, Inc. have some suggestions regarding the purchase of firearms and recommend the following items:

AR 15 (M4 Style) piston driven with heavy barrel stamped 223/5.56 Nato. Please note that the 223 and 5.56 are not the same round and a barrel that is stamped 223 is not adequate for shooting 5.56 round, but the reverse is not true. Shoot whatever your barrel is stamped that is the bottom line. However, the heavy barrel can shoot both. This rifle is about $1,500 -2,000k.

SKS – You can find a SKS from $300-$400 in good working condition. These rifles are better then the AK 47. They have a longer heaver barrel which makes the rifle have less recoil, shoot longer and allows the person shooting to be more accurate. Plus they are piston driven.

Mini 14 (Ruger) – You can find these rifles in Walmarts or local gun shops everywhere. They cost about $600.00 and are a 223 caliber with 20 round magazines. This is considered a ranch rifle but has great multi-functions that are possible. If you are looking for a 223 caliber that is cheap this is the one, it has a great reputation for durability.

Sig Suar (9mm or 45 cal) Sig has a great reputation but the cost can be considerably more than other handguns.

Glock / Springfield XD (9mm or 45 cal) – I personally went with the XD over the Glock in 45 cal and 4" barrel. I found that through my research this weapon had everything I wanted and was less expensive then its counterparts. Best of all for those with little ones around – in the 45 cal it comes with a thumb safety. The thumb safety was the deciding factor for me. For me the 45 caliber is the ideal caliber with enough to get the job done with one shot -it is a true combat caliber.

Browning's X-Bolt Varmint Stalker – Seems to be the best bang for the buck for long-range weapons in bolt action. We recommend a 308 caliber weapon as it is the most versatile or the long range rounds. It will also be the most common round for long range snipers.

AR 15 in 308 Caliber with heavy barrel – a nice alternative for those wanting a large caliber and high mag capacity.

Self-Defense Training

As some of you may know the American Christian Defense Alliance Inc. started out as a Martial Arts Ministry in hopes of ministering to those who would not enter a church building as well as to disciple fellow brothers and sisters in Christ in proper doctrine. Therefore, it should come as no surprise to those reading this book that the American Christian Defense Alliance highly advocates self-defense training in any preparedness planning.

Consider this, knowledge is power and the knowledge and the skill that you possess to defend you and your family could potentially be the difference maker in a life-and-death situation. Whether you're a radical Muslim terrorists or just some thug you're not going to want to deal with someone or attack someone that has the skills necessary to defend themselves in a real way.

Individuals such as thugs or radical Muslim terrorists normally attempt to attack what they perceive to be as soft targets. A soft target can be defined as a target that will offer little resistance in the process of the attacker victimizing them and offer little if any in the way of defense. This is why thugs here in America walk around in groups sometimes they are gangs other times they are not, nevertheless they attack in numbers because they are cowards. Just like radical Muslim terrorists attack soft targets such as public transportation, again which offer little if any in the way of security.

So for the Christian Prepper where does one begin - one begins first and foremost with physical fitness. I mean this with no disrespect when I say this - but if you are fat, lazy, or out of shape you are most likely incapable of doing what is necessary to defend yourself or your family from groups that attack and that my friend you will be accountable for before God.

Our bodies are the temples of the Holy Spirit - The indwelling of the Spirit of God and we must respect our bodies and train them accordingly.

There are lots of ways the Christian Prepper can get in physical shape but it all starts with a mindset, the very will and determination to see things through to the end. This type of discipline is very rare in today's world especially for those that call themselves Christian.

Nevertheless, a great place to start would be to start eating right. Removing all fast food from your diet would be an excellent choice as well as eating organic foods as best as possible.

Some may argue to eliminate meat altogether from your diet. I would disagree with this as our bodies are designed to be meat eaters, however, I would limit your meat consumption to beef, chicken, lamb, fish, or rabbits – in other words try to stay away from the pork as its difficult to digest.

There are plenty other options out there with wild game or in the grocery store to choose rather than ingesting pork into your body.

Water should of probably been first on the list regarding eating right. Water is the one thing on the planet that you absolutely need - yet if you look at our tap water with the fluoride and other chemicals within it, any reasonable person would conclude it's probably not a good idea to drink it. Stay away from tap water even if you purify it, filter it, or boil it – stay away. There are just too many things they are putting in the water nowadays and to be quite honest they probably don't even tell us everything that's in it.

With that in mind I would highly recommend drinking spring water that has been filtered and purified through a drip type filter.

There are several of these types of filters to choose from, each one has its pros and cons. If you're looking for a filter for everyday use within your home stick to a stainless steel model and one that has a ceramic filter. Some ceramic filters are impregnated with silver, which is an awesome thing. Silver acts as a natural antibacterial agent and keeps the actual filter as clean as possible.

The filter that I personally have is the pro-pure one. I have used the Berkey Sport model previously but did not care for the build up of slimy residue on the plastic containers. I also found that unlike the ceramic filters the carbon-based filters that are black also developed the same slimy residue. Again stick to stainless steel and ceramic filters.

Once you establish the diet that consist of higher-quality foods and remove the genetically modified foods from you and your family's life you will feel a lot healthier and begin a lifelong process learning how to eat properly.

After this established it's important to get into an exercise routine. Now for the Christian Prepper I don't recommend just any exercise routine but an exercise routine that is based on real-world application of self-defense methods. This is where we get into different styles of martial arts. Each style has different benefits to offer the end-user. However, there's only a few established styles that I know of that offer real-world self preservation techniques from a Christian perspective.

There are styles out there such as the Israeli self-defense system called Krav Maga that are established combat systems. This is a combat system with the proper mindset yet lacks Jesus Christ as its fundamental anchor and lacks the Word of God as a guiding moral principle. Now yes, this is a bit of the plug for our self-defense ministry called Seisho Ryu Goshin-Jutsu here.

Our self-defense system incorporates the proper combat mindset as well as a Christian or Biblical foundation for its moral compass. I encourage each of you to find out more about our particular martial arts ministry and style by visiting our website online.

Chapter 8: Kits & Bags

If you spend any time at all around prepping or survivalist circles, you're going to end up hearing people talk about their various types of kits and bags. That's basically because of the importance of having everything you need with you to survive is so critical. While it is theoretically possible to survive without a kit, it is infinitely harder and requires much more knowledge about survival. Jesus Himself told His Disciples to go sell what you have and buy a bag . . .

Luke: 22: 35-38:
(35) And He said to them, "When I sent you without money bag, knapsack, and sandals, did you lack anything?" so they said, "Nothing." (36) Then He said to them, "But now, he who has a money bag, let him take it, and likewise a knapsack; and he who has no sword, let him sell his garment and buy one. (37) For I say to you that this which is written must still be accomplished in Me:

'And He was numbered with the transgressors. For the things concerning Me have an end." (38) So they said, "Lord, look, here are two swords." And He said to them, "It is enough."

Why is this so important? Well, Jesus Himself mentioned the need to get out and away from the city, in times of calamity. His answer was to go to the mountains. Escape and Evade is the concept . . . God says flee to the mountains and don't go back to get anything – therefore, watch and pray and be ready at all times: Matt. 24:15-20 / Mark 13

Mark 13: 14 -19 ["So when you see the 'abomination of desolation, spoken of by Daniel the prophet, standing where it ought not" (let the reader understand), "then let those who are in Judea flee to the mountains. Let him who is on the housetop not go down into the house, nor enter to take anything out of his house. And let him who is in the field not go back to get his clothes. But woe to those who are pregnant and to those who are nursing babies in those days!

And pray that your flight may not be in winter. For in those days there will be tribulation, such as has not been since the beginning of the creation which God created until this time, nor ever shall be.]

But if you're going to do that, you need to go prepared as much as possible. The problem for many people is trying to figure out what all those different bag names mean and what you actually need to have in them so you can survive. So, let's look at the various types of kits and bags you might encounter:

Survival kit - This is a small, portable kit, usually packed into something the size of a hardcover book or smaller. The idea is to have something with you at all times, that gives you the essentials for survival. Many people carry these while hiking, or keep one in their car.

EDC Bag (Everyday Carry Bag) - The EDC is intended to give you everything you would need to have with you, if a disaster happened and you were away from home. As such, it needs to cover a lot of ground in a fairly small package. A typical EDC is roughly the size of a lunch box, although the shape can vary greatly. In many cases, people add non-essential, but useful things to their EDC, such as stamps, safety pins, and a phone charger.

Get Home Bag - The idea behind a get home bag is to provide you with enough urban survival equipment and a little food, so that you can make it home from work, in the event of a disaster. The assumption is that you would have to walk, so a get home bag may even include a good pair of walking shoes. Properly done, a EDC can also be used as a get home bag.

But Out Bag (BOB) - Sometimes called a 72-hour bag, this is what you would use if you determine you need to bug out and get away from home to survive a disaster. Different people's BOB will hold different equipment, depending on their bug out plan. It is intended to get you to your survival shelter, whether that is in another city, a cabin in the woods, or if you are going to live off the land. Obviously, if you're going to live off the land, you need more survival gear.

Inch Bag - This is the extreme version of a bug out bag, for those who intend to live off the land for the rest of their lives. Inch stands for "I'm never coming back." As the name implies, that means you're going to need a lot of gear to make it through.

Regardless of the type of bag, they all have to provide for the basic survival needs, which are:

- A way to maintain your body temperature
- Clean water
- Food
- Fire
- Self-defense
- First-aid

Portability is an important consideration. You can't assume that you'll be able to use your car. Roads may be impassible, so you'll have to head out on foot. If that's the case, you want your kit or bag to be something that you can take with you. That means putting it into a portable pack, such as a backpack or over-the-shoulder bag that you can actually carry. Therefore, you also need to consider how much weight you can carry, especially in the cases of the bug out bag and inch bag.

Chapter 9: The EDC

What is an Every Day Carry (EDC)? Disasters, like babies being born, show up on when they want, not when we want. That generally means at the most inopportune times. Somethings probably not going to happen when you're at your home and have just finished repacking your bug-out bag. It'll happen when you least expect it and aren't anywhere near your survival equipment.

That's why you need to be carrying some basic things with you every single day. If you walk out your door, you need to have enough with you to make it back home. Now, that doesn't mean you need to take your bug out bag with you, but it does mean that you need some things.

The idea of Ever Day Carry (EDC) is to have the essentials with you. We can break this down into two levels; the essentials that you carry on your person and those that you carry in an EDC bag.

The difference is, there are times when you will put your EDC bag down, such as while you are at work. Most would probably leave their EDC bag in the car while working; but the items you carry on your person are those that you might need in a matter of seconds, rather than minutes.

So, what are these items that you might need in seconds?

- Pistol with extra ammo (not only to defend yourself, but to defend others; believers should take a stand to protect the weak)
- Good knife and/or multi-tool with a knife blade
- Fire starter (a butane lighter works well for this)
- Flashlight
- Cash
- Keys
- Smartphone (have survival manuals and an electronic Bible in memory)
- Tactical pen (a pen which can also be used as a hand held weapon)
- Analog watch (an analog watch can be used as a compass, a digital can't)

As you can see, these items are more focused on self-defense and getting out of your workplace, than they are anything else. The idea isn't so much allowing you to survive in the woods, or even survive sleeping in a cardboard box as you walk home from a disaster. Those items are in your Every Day Carry (EDC) kit. But there are some things that happen so quickly, that waiting till you get to your car just won't work.

If a terrorist or lunatic enters your workplace and starts shooting the place up, you don't have time to go to your car to get your gun. You need to be able to react in seconds. Likewise, if the lights go out, you'll need a flashlight on your person, not in your Every Day Carry (EDC) kit. That's the type of criteria that are used to select these items.

But it's clear that the Every Day Carry (EDC) items listed above aren't going to be enough to get you home, if you have to walk home after an EMP renders your car unusable or some other disaster happens. There are also many other things that can happen in a day, which really don't qualify as emergencies. Carrying a few basics in your Every Day Carry (EDC) to take care of those little problems is always a great idea.

Every Day Carry (EDC) bags can vary greatly in size, but for most people they're about the size of a lunch box or large fanny pack. I use an over the shoulder bag, but you can use anything.

This gives me quite a bit of room for the things I feel I need.

- Shelter - 2 rescue blankets, 20' of para-cord and 10 yd of duct tape
- Rain poncho
- Lifestraw
- Nalgene water bottle
- Some high energy snacks, such as beef jerky, granola bars and nuts
- Spork - useful for those times when my lunch doesn't come with utensils
- Fire starter - I carry a lighter, as well as a BlastMatch Jr. and some WetFire cubes
- Flashlight and spare batteries
- Knife (in addition to the one in my pocket)
- Wire saw
- Compass and map - to help me find my way home
- Lock pick set (ssh!)
- Phone charger - includes cable, adapters for wall and car, as well as a charger battery
- Hair bands - useful as rubber bands for a number of things
- Emergency sewing kit - for quick repairs, heavy on safety pins
- Pen, pencil and waterproof pad
- Photocopies of my driver's license and passport

- Personal hygiene kit - includes antibacterial hand cleaner, disposable toothbrushes, deodorant, 3 compressed towels and Kleenex (can be used as toilet paper)
- First-aid - cloth bandages of various types, abdominal bandages (large bandages) alcohol wipes, cohesive medical tape, antibacterial ointment, pain relievers, antihistamine, 3 day supply of my personal medications, clotting compound and butterfly closures

With this, I have enough to get myself home from pretty much anywhere within walking distance, as well as take care of the problems which might arise during the day. If your work requires you to dress in a way that is not conducive for walking, add good walking shoes and some more comfortable clothes. Always carry a jacket with you, even on days when you don't need it. You might need it at night.

Chapter 10: The Bug Out Bag

When the time comes to bug out, you're going to need equipment and supplies to survive; that's where the bug out bag comes in. You're not going to be able to go to someplace where you can pick up a loaf of bread and a gallon of milk at the corner store. Nor are you likely to find an abandoned cabin in the woods, with a welcome sign hanging on the door.

You're going to have to live off of what you take with you, the knowledge you have and what nature provides. So, it's best to take as much with you as possible while keeping in mind weight, specifically the things that will help you survive out in the wild long-term. Of course, that means knowing how to use those things to survive with as well. Ultimately, the most important thing you can take with you is the knowledge of how to survive.

The bug out bag must provide for all of your basic needs, so it would be a good idea to review what those are. In order of priority, your needs are:

- Safety & Security
- Maintaining your body heat (this includes clothing, shelter and fire)
- Purified water
- Food
- First-aid (including personal hygiene)

Carrying all of that is going to be a bit difficult. You have to assume that you're going to have to go on foot at some point. Even if you leave home in your car or truck, chances are that you'll have to abandon it along the way. With that in mind, you need to make your bug out bag something that you can carry, such as a backpack. While other things can be used, a backpack is your best bet.

When selecting a backpack, try to avoid something that is obviously military in appearance. That's too easy to identify as what it is. You don't want people to realize that you're bugging out or recognize that you're prepared. So, you're better off with a backpacker's backpack, rather than a military one.

At the same time, if you find yourself in a combat situation prior to heading out a military backpack of some kind may not be a bad option because it is designed with combat as its primary task. You will need something rugged and durable regardless.

Also you'll want to make sure that whatever backpack you pick has a weight-bearing belt. Your legs are much stronger than your back, and can support the weight of the backpack and its contents easier than your back can. But if the pack doesn't have a belt, your back will have to carry the weight and that's a serious no, no.

Most people have to limit their pack to about one-fourth their body weight. But that's assuming that you're in shape. If not, you'll have to make it even less. One way to compensate for this is to have every member of the family carry their own pack. While women and children can't carry as big or heavy a pack as a man can, they should be able to carry their own clothes, personal toiletries and sleeping bag, as well as some of the communal food.

Bug out bags are very personal, simply because each person's situation is unique. You need to match the pack you carry to your needs, the terrain you are going to travel through, the area you are going to set up camp and your own survival skills. There's absolutely no sense in carrying equipment you can't use, no matter how useful it might seem. Additionally don't forget to leave room for weapons and ammunition – this is one of the most over looked areas of so called experts who advise on building Bug Out Bags.

Safety and Security should be the number one thing to consider in your preparedness because without security you will no doubt be a victim in some way, shape, or form.

One small great option to consider for perimeter security is a 12 gage alert. This small item can be attached to a tree and loaded with a blank 12 gage round. When a person or animal walks past and trips the wire it will go off.

Now because of the nature of this device and the legality of such I have to through out a disclaimer to use according to all Federal, State, and local laws. Also please be advised that if you add any type of actual "Live Rounds" even less then lethal rounds you will be breaking some serious Federal laws – Do you own research prior to modifying this device in anyway and only use it according to its indented purpose. Now if SHTF is occurring and the United States is no longer a functional government you may want to re-evaluate things based on the current dynamics going on. Again Your Decision, Your Responsibilities, and Your possible Consequences.

Chapter 11: The INCH Bag

An INCH Bag – That Sounds Tiny . . .
. What is an INCH Bag?

Most of us understand what a Bug Out Bag is unless we've been living in an isolated situation. Bug Out Bags come in all shapes and styles. Some of the commercial ones are heavy on food and water, with only a little bit of basic survival gear included. On the other end of the spectrum, we find Bug Out Bags that have every survival gadget and goodie you can imagine. This wide discrepancy raises a lot of questions in people's minds, especially people who are new to prepping.

The thing is, different people have different ideas of prepping and different ideas of bugging out. The simpler bug out bags are based on FEMA's recommended list, from their emergency preparedness website. But that list assumes that anyone bugging out is going to head for their nearest FEMA shelter to ride out the disaster.

Well, I don't know about you, but turning myself over to the government is not something that I'm willing to do.

That's why my Bug Out Bag is really an INCH bag. That means "I'm Not Coming Home" bag. Does that mean that if I Bug Out, I'm never coming back? To be honest, I don't know. But I pack that bag as if that's the case, because there's no way for me to know.

You've probably seen some of those movies about the End Times, where a small group of believers is hiding out from the government and society in general. Well, what would you need, if you were in that situation? A regular bug out bag wouldn't be enough, because you would be leaving home, without the idea of ever coming back.

An INCH bag has to be heavy on survival gear, as it may very well contain all your worldly possessions, once you leave your home.

If your home is destroyed and you are forced to abandon it, you could literally end up with that being everything you own. In that case, it needs to have everything you'll need while on the move.

What does that mean? It means that your INCH bag will contain enough tools and equipment that you can build a long-term shelter, start innumerable fires and filter your own water, as well as hunt and scavenge for your own food. At the same time, you're going to have to be your own doctor, provide yourself with clothing, make shoes and make anything else you're going to need. That's going to be one packed bag.

In reality, you can't fit all that in one backpack; at least, not and still be able to carry it. What you really need is more than one bag. The first one is your bug out bag, and it contains all your survival equipment.

The second (and possibly third) bags will contain:

- Extra clothing
- Sleeping bags
- Ammo
- Hunting bow (with arrows)
- Seeds

Those contents are going to have to be able to help you start your homestead off in the wild. Seeds and a hunting bow are very important parts of this list, as they will give you the ability to feed yourself, without attracting attention. While a nice hunting rifle is easier to hunt with, it's also noisy. Bows may not have as long a range, but at least they're quiet.

You can build a long-term shelter with the tools you can carry in a Bug Out Bag, but it's gonna be hard. That's why I mention tools in the second bag. Those tools will be the tools you'll use to build a shelter. If you have the skills to use them consider the following tools list for specifically building a long-term shelter

Tools you may need:
- Shovel
- Full-sized axe
- Bow saw or bucksaw
- Froe (for making shingles and splitting boards)
- Adze (for squaring tops and bottoms of logs for a cabin, as well as making furniture)
- Framing chisel
- Carpenter's crosscut saw
- Pick (for breaking up ground)
- Brace & bits (for drilling holes)

I realize that sounds like a rather extensive tool list and it represents a lot of weight. But if you're going to build a log cabin out in the woods somewhere, that's the minimum you're going to need unless your just that skilled with an axe and buck saw. As it is, you're going to do a lot of backbreaking work with those tools, in order to get your cabin built. If you leave anything out, you're going to have a much harder time of it.

Chapter 12:
The Bug Out Vehicle (BOV)

The Bug Out Vehicle for Christian Preppers – What's that All about? For many preppers, Bug Out vehicles are one of the "fun" parts of prepping. I mean, c'mon, who doesn't want a nice big four-wheel-drive pickup, all decked out for fun in the rocks and the mud? There's just something manly about that image, like an untamed stallion running across the prairie. We all want to be that one who catches and tames that stallion… or truck… or whatever.

But before you run out and sign a huge loan for that big truck you're wanting, let's stop and think about it for a moment. You want to be sure to get the right thing, especially on such a big purchase. New trucks are expensive, especially new four-wheel-drive trucks. Before you can even start picking out a bug out vehicle, you need to develop your bug out plan.

That means knowing where you're going to go, the triggers that will tell you it's time to go and how you're going to get there. Once you have that, you're ready to start thinking about your bug out vehicle.

Some people get real elaborate with their bug out vehicles, buying or building something that's more suited for the military, than for a family. While I like those vehicles as much as the next guy, I'm not sure that they're a practical selection for a bug out vehicle. Oh, they'll get you there… at least, if the crowd of people on the freeway don't stop you and kill you for your vehicle.

You see, stealth is an important part of Bugging Out, as important as mobility. You have to assume that other people are going to be Bugging Out at the same time and that traffic will get backed up. When that happens, there's a good chance that some vehicles will run out of gas and others will overheat.

Their owners will become desperate and start looking for anything they can find to help them out of the situation. In such a moment, your fancy 4×4 truck, could look like salvation to them.

The last thing you want to do is put yourself in the position where you either have to kill someone or allow them to kill you. While that may end up happening anyway, you should try and avoid it. Killing is still killing, and while the law may not be around to catch you, God's law will always be there and judge accordingly.

Of course, a lot depends on where you live. In Texas, just about everyone drives a truck or SUV. So yours won't stand out. But if you're driving that in New York, it probably will. So, pick a vehicle that will blend in and make sure it's in a color that won't attract attention.

The flip side of that coin is being able to go off-road, if you need to. There's a good chance that all those out of gas and overheated vehicles will end up blocking the highways. When that happens, it might be necessary to cut across some empty field or even some farmer's field, in order to get away. You're not going to do that successfully in your average family sedan.

Only you can analyze your escape route and determine if four-wheel-drive will really help you. If it won't then there's no real reason to buy it. You've got to balance that against your need for stealth, as well as thinking about how much space you need for your family and what you're going to take with you.

In all actuality, you probably already have a vehicle that you can use as a Bug Out vehicle. Maybe it won't be as good and maybe it won't be as sexy; but taking out a loan to buy a Bug Out vehicle, which will prevent you from doing the other prepping you need, isn't a wise use of your money. Take the time to think it through and make sure that your plan ends up fitting your budget.

Chapter 13:
The Bug Out Retreat (BOR)

A Bug Out Retreat – That doesn't sound like it make sense. Preppers regularly debate the wisdom of bugging out versus bugging in, with the majority of experts coming down on the side of bugging in. But that's based on some very clear assumptions, especially the assumption that anyone bugging out is going to go live in the wild, trying to live off the land with nothing but what they're carrying in their bug out bag.

Based on that assumption, I'd have to say that bugging in is preferable. Living off the land is much harder than most of us realize. But that doesn't make bugging in an excellent idea, especially if you live in a big city. Even disasters as small as a hurricane can cause a breakdown in society, at least to some extent. If that's the case, then what's going to happen with a major disaster? Say, something nationwide?

The lawless element of society will grow and they'll be attacking anyone they can, in order to find the things that they need to have in order to survive. Being a prepper around such people will become very dangerous.

That's why a bug out retreat is a superior option to bugging in. A bug out retreat gives you the option of leaving town and getting away from the two-legged predators, without having to put your family at risk. By pre-planning and preparing someplace to go, you can best protect your family. But there's another reason for us to bug out, rather than bug in. That is, Jesus gave us that advice. In fact, He tells us that in three of the gospels (Mt 24:16; Mar 13:14; Luke 21:21), which means it must be important. Specifically, he tells us to go to the mountains when we see the abomination of desolation. So, where are there mountains nearby you?

Hold on, I can already hear you. There are some of you out there saying that you can't afford a bug out retreat. Maybe that's true or maybe you're just thinking of it the wrong way. Buying the land is usually the most expensive part. If you can get away from that part, you can take out a lot of the cost of building your bug out retreat. In fact, that opens a number of possibilities to you.

The first of these is to create it on property owned by a friend or family member who lives out of town. Perhaps their reason for living outside of town is that they want to survive. If that's the case, you can form a survival team together. Then, you can build a shelter on their property out of scavenged materials. Another option is to use a travel trailer. You can buy older used travel trailers for a couple thousand dollars. If you're the do-it-yourselfer type, you can fix that trailer up, making a nice shelter out of it. Then you either keep it at home or find a good place to store it, that would be conveniently close to where you plan on placing your bug out shelter.

Don't forget small towns either. Most of them will be much safer during a crisis than the big cities. But people who live in small towns will probably be suspicious of strangers. So, you will need to integrate yourself with that town beforehand, so that they accept you when you arrive. Regardless of the type of bug out retreat you create, the mountains are the best place to do it. Not only will you be well hidden from those two-legged predators, but the mountains provide an abundance of resources which you will need to have access to, in order to survive.

Chapter 14: Caching

Caches? What in the World are Caches; is that like a peanut? No, No that a Cashew. If you are still reading at Chapter 14 you may know what Caches are, but how much do you really know? One common mistake for Preppers to make is to keep their entire stockpile in their home, in one location or in one cache. On one hand, that makes sense, as most people plan on bugging in during a disaster, rather than bugging out.

But on the other hand, having everything in your home or one location means that in the case of a disaster that destroys your home, or in the case of a mob attacking your stockpiled location, you lose everything you have – And the wife is not going to like that one bit, especially when she most likely put up with your crazy prepping for so long. Now when it's needed the most it's not there – Yea, definitely not going to go over well.

That's why supply caches are so important. They spread your supplies around, putting them in convenient places where you might need them. That way, no matter what you end up having to do to survive a disaster, you have some supplies readily at hand. Now these supplies will not be very extensive most likely but will give you what you need to hand on and survive.

To accomplish this, you need caches in multiple locations. While that is more work, it will ultimately serve you better to have several different caches which you can access, rather than just one – And the wife can be happy. Basically, you want to break your caches down into a few basic areas:

Near your home – If you are bugging in, you want extra supplies that you can access readily. These caches also serve if your home is broken into and your supplies are stolen or your home is destroyed and you need some ready supplies. Local storage units are great for this – But think Creatively

Your workplace – If you own your own business or you have some storage space available at your work, you could create a small cache there. That would provide you with supplies for yourself and your co-workers, if a disaster leaves you trapped at work for a few days.

Your bug-out location – This is probably the most important place to have caches prepared. You probably won't be able to take everything you need with you, so by having caches at or near your bug out location, you ensure that you will have supplies available. If you own that location, you can stock it well, but if not, you'll need to find someplace to hide your caches.

Along your bug out route – The average bug out bag only has three to five days worth of food in it. But if you have to go on foot, you may need many more days to get to your survival retreat than the food you are carrying. Putting a couple of caches along the way allows you to re-supply. You should do this every 3-5 Miles, especially if you're traveling with children.

Combat Caches – This is something you should consider wisely and as I must mention in accordance with all local, state, and federal laws. Combat Caches are designed to give you a tactical advantage and could be stocked with a multitude of items that include things like sealed ammo, parts to firearms, knives, etc. – Just use your imagination but stay within the law. Combat Caches should be placed in a tactically advantageous location such as high ground, rocky terrain, vantage points, etc.

Cashes . . . Closing Remarks

As you can see, properly placing a cache requires considerable forethought. You need to pick locations that are going to work out well as part of your overall survival plan. Not just anyplace will do. But where do you actually make the cache?

One of the best locations I've run across for a survival cache is a rented storage locker; the kind that has sprung up all across the country as people's possessions outgrew their storage space. You can rent small spaces the size of a closet, for a minimal monthly fee, which is enough space to set up a pretty good cache.

Another option is to establish one at the home of a like-minded friend or family member, if they have space. Of course, they'll have to be someone you can trust.

The other possibility is to bury your caches. This is best for the ones along your bug out route and may also be best at your bug out location. Plastic five-gallon buckets work well for this, as they are water-tight, can hold a fair amount and are readily available at all home improvement centers. You can also use PVC pipe, but that won't hold as much.

If you bury caches, make sure that you have multiple landmarks to locate them by. Don't use trees for landmarks, as they can burn down or be cut down. Instead, use features of the landscape, such as rock outcroppings. Those are permanent, short of removing them with heavy equipment or dynamite. If that becomes the case, you'll probably lose your cache anyway.

You can put literally anything in a cache, but the basic idea is to use them for food, ammunition and basic survival equipment.

You should already have your survival equipment with you, so the only reason I'm mentioning survival equipment is in case you lose yours or can't get to your bug out bag. Other than that, the biggest item is food, as that's what you'll be consuming the most of.

Chapter 15:
Alternative Housing Options

Now there are two options – Stay put and dig in or Bug Out. As we already clarified in a previous chapter God's plan is for us to Bug Out so we can avoid being a victim of circumstances. Have you ever realized that God always provides a way of escape for His people, whether it's an Ark, Rapture, or Mighty Man of God to lead His people – He always provides a way of escape.

Tiny Houses may seem to be the next Big Thing but are they right for the Christian Prepper? Tiny Houses offer a lot of options but they are still stationary. I don't consider the Tiny Houses on Trailers actually Tiny Houses. When I talk about Tiny Houses I'm talking about a small shed like building that is on the ground – just so we are on the same page here. It makes sense why so many people considering them.

Many are sick of the rat race and are actively taking steps to ensure their future survival both economically and beyond. It is absolutely possible to have a Tiny House built for 10-20k that has enough room for you and your family's needs.

If you put it on some land .... you're good to go. For some that might make a good Bug Out Retreat. Others might consider this option if they have special needs or situations such as an ill family member. However, if at all possible actively consider a mobile lifestyle – This is the Biblical example.

RVing Full-Time may be the way to go. I gotta say hitting the open road and not looking back does sound very appealing right now with the way our country is. I actually believe that the American Christian who can do RVing full-time should do so. I believe God calls us to use "Escape & Evasion" tactics in these last day when we will be hunted and killed in the 5th Seal. Start the process today.

Chapter 16: Alternative Energy Options

Alternative Energy Options for the Christian Prepper... Do we really need to worry about Alternative Energy Options as a Christian while Bugging Out? However, what if we're not on the Bugging Out and like most experience a power outage do to a storm or disaster that wasn't expected? We have to plan for multiple scenarios at the same time to truly be prepared. It's not all just about the End of Days. Let's think about a few things...

In pretty much any disaster, there's one thing in common; a loss of electrical power. In fact, it doesn't even take a true disaster to cause a power outage. A spring thunderstorm or a buildup of ice in the winter can bring down power lines, leaving people without power.

Our electrical grid is aging. Some parts are over 100 years old. But it was only designed to last 50 years. So, it's not surprising that winter storms and more serious disasters can all cause serious problems with the grid.

But with modern society's dependence upon electricity for almost everything, this loss of power can have grave consequences, especially if it takes more than a few hours to restore.

The only security any of us can have against the loss of power is being able to generate our own. Even limited electrical generation capability, while not enough to operate everything in our homes, will allow us to operate some critical systems, keeping our food from spoiling, maintaining communications, operating the many small electronics we use every day, providing ourselves with light and operating medical equipment that family members might need.

While there are many different ways of generating electrical power, there are really only three that are practical for most people to use. Others are either too expensive or require special circumstances, such as a private river to erect a water wheel. For most these three are sufficient:

Gas Generator – While the most common means of producing electrical power in an emergency, gas generators are actually the least efficient.

The high cost of fuel to operate the generator quickly overcomes the savings in buying the equipment. However, if one has a limited budget to spend on electrical generation, a gas generator is the least expensive to buy.

Solar Panels – Solar has become the "go to" method for home power generation. Sunlight is a plentiful resource in most of the country, so there is no shortage of fuel to power the system.

However, it is the most expensive to buy and install. You can mitigate this cost by building your own, saving about half the price of commercially manufactured systems. The cost of the system is also offset by the fact that it has zero operating cost.

Wind Turbine – Wind power has become a popular alternative for green energy companies. It is cheaper to build than solar and produces more power. However, wind only produces electricity when you have winds that are over ten miles per hour. So, it doesn't work well in all parts of the country. Like solar, you can save a considerable amount of money building your own.

The best is to integrate systems, together, such as having some solar and a wind turbine. That way, there is power being produced, regardless of the weather.

A fully integrated system should also have a battery bank, with the solar panels and wind turbine charging the batteries and power being drawn off the batteries to power the electronic devices needed in the home. While a fairly hefty additional cost, this ensures that there is always electrical power available in the home.

When looking at alternative power systems for use in an emergency, keep in mind that it isn't necessary to create enough electricity to power everything in your home. All you need is enough for your essential systems, such as those mentioned above. Creating a system that powers your whole home or RV needs is inherently expensive. If you would like more information on Alternative Energy Options check out some of the links below.

Alternative Energy Options for the Christian Prepper:

- Sun Jack
- Renology
- Goal Zero

Chapter 17: What to Buy
A Basic Shopping List for Your BOB

Basic Tools for your Bug out Bag:
Concept: Never rely completely on one particular item to get a job done!

- Back Pack
- Your Weapons & Ammo (a Ruger 10/22 or Shotgun is a Great Choice for general survival but will only help a little when dealing with the two legged bad guys – for that consider the AR15, AK, or SKS.
- Good Knife (The Best You Can Afford)
- Multi-Function Tool (Gerber or Leatherman)
- Folding Saw (Bahco Laplander)
- Bob's Quick Buck Saw (with extra blades)
- One Gransfors Bruks Axe
- Cold Steel Special Forces Shovel
- 550 Cord 300 feet and number 12 Bank Line (1lb spoil)

Shelter:

- Small 2 person Tent. This is actually a one-person tent with your gear. If you have a family plan accordingly. However, just remember to stay out of sight. Reusable Space Emergency Blanket / Tarp
- SOL Emergency Bivy – Green
- United States Military Bivy is another option. This is more durable but add a little more weight.
- One 100% Wool Blanket. Make sure it's actually 100% wool.

Fire Starting Equipment:

- Faro Rod
- Magnifying Glass
- Flint & Steel
- Metal Container holding Card Cloth
- Magnesium Block
- Matches in water proof container of some kind
- Lighters

- Cotton Balls covered in petroleum jelly
- Knowledge and Ability to start fire using primitive techniques such as the bow and drill & hand drill and Modern Techniques of using Batteries to start fires.

Food:

- Cliff Bars (20 grams of Protein each)
- Organic Trail Mix
- 1 Mainstay Food Ration Bar (3600 cal.)
- 3-5 MREs (because you don't need water to cook them)
- Snares, Fishing Yo Yos, and two 220 Conibear Traps
- The Ability to catch, trap, or hunt game to secure a renewable food source as well as process it in the field. Don't forget to bring some zip lock bags. Learn how to smoke you meats to help preserve it.

Water:

- Purification Tablets
- Water Filter (Katadyn Pocket Micro filter)
- 1 Plastic fold-down 5 gallon water container
- 1 Steel cup/bowl for boiling water (Stanley put out a really good little kit)
- Knowledge and Ability to gather and create safe drinking water through creating a Solar Still, Survival Filter, and Boiling Water

Documents:

- Small Bible
- Small copy of Declaration of Independence and US Constitution with Bill of Rights
- Small survival field book
- And of course maps of locations you will be traveling in.

Chapter 18: Personal Care

In chapter 7 I briefly discussed proper food and water, in this chapter we will cover personal care as it relates to bugging out. Additionally we will cover hygiene while bugging out and medical training you should receive prior to having to bug out.

Hygiene and Personal Care

Hygiene and personal care while bugging out is something of critical importance. Hygiene and personal care is the number one issue taking people out worldwide. Even more than war improper hygiene and personal care is one of the fastest ways to take you and your family out of the game. Therefore it's important to plan and prep accordingly. Those with special needs should take great care and caution in the planning as medications and urgent care most likely will not be available. There are options to stock up on antibiotics if that's something you are in need of through the use of fish antibiotics. However, use at your own discretion and accordingly to all applicable laws.

The label itself will tell you this is only for fish. A great Christian Prepper who just also happens to be a nurse did a great video on this a while back just search out the Patriot Nurse on YouTube. She does a lot of great videos on medical preparedness and does offer classes throughout the country. If you do stop by and visit her let her know you found her through our book.

One of the main things to throw into your bug out bag is a personal care kit. This kit should include things such as tweezers, toenail clippers, a pair of scissors, a bandanna and other individual specific hygiene items. Again remember stores are not open so what you have is what you have and you need to be able to improvise with what you bring. Women especially should take note of this and plan accordingly to deal with her menstrual cycle.

Medical Training

At the bare minimum every adult should be trained in First Aid and CPR. Medical training should be completed prior to any situation taking place if at all possible.

Do not put off medical training, as you do not know when a situation will take place in which you may need this particular training. I personally am an American Red Cross Instructor and have taught numerous individuals first aid and CPR classes at different places I've worked. I continue to offer training to those within our organization.

This training is on a first-come first serve basis and is limited to 10 people per class. In the future the American Christian defense Alliance, Inc. hopes to offer further courses from the American Red Cross. Their training is top-notch and very professional.

Conclusion

The conclusion of this book is actually the beginning of your journey. Now is the time to take massive action and get things done again not out of the spirit of fear, but out of the spirit of love using your sound mind that God has given you. We will all go through different spurts and times in which we feel anxious, worried or fearful and these are the times that try men's souls - yet as you cling ever closer to Christ and His word you will have the peace of God that surpasses all understanding for God cannot lie when he promises in His Word is an unstoppable truth.

We have covered a lot of subjects throughout this book yet to be quite honest we've only scratched the surface. I hope that you use this book as it's intended, for the purpose of this book is for you and your family to get prepared as best as possible from a Christian perspective, to give you the operational framework that is necessary instead of going through all of the craziness to put the pieces of the puzzle together – I hope in some small way this helps put the pieces of the puzzle together that much quicker for you and that you truly gain the necessary understanding that God wants for you. For God does not desire for His people to be ignorant – what does the word of God say, my people perish for lack of knowledge. God doesn't want His people to perish but to have an intimate personal relationship with Him through understanding the Word of God.

I hope you will also pass on this book to potentially a nonbeliever in Jesus Christ who may be receptive to information regarding prepping and preparedness – again our greatest prep, our greatest asset if you would in our life should be Jesus Christ and even now I still implore you to come to Jesus right now while you yet still can, while there is still hope for change in Christ Jesus, while you yet still have breath in your lungs to speak the words that can bring everlasting healing, hope, peace, and everlasting life – do it now my friend. For God said in an acceptable time I've heard your cry and helped you - behold now is the time for salvation, behold now is the time.

This is the American Christian Defense Alliance, Inc. attempt to help warn and prepare you before it's too late – We have done our part, Now what will you do?

Special Gift

God has a Gift for You!　The Plan of Salvation:

There is no formal prayer of salvation as many churches would have you believe, God's Word is very clear - there is only one way to get to the Father in heaven and that is through Jesus Christ (John 14:6). Jesus says that you must be born again to enter into heaven (John 3:3-5).

Salvation is simply the first step in building an open and honest relationship with God. We all have sinned and fallen short, but there is Hope in Jesus Christ - Just cry out to God in sincerity and honesty asking for forgiveness and for Him to Save you, Sanctify you, and fill you with His Holy Spirit - Ask for His will to be done in your life on earth as it is in Heaven and That's it, now just keep it real with God.

A Warning:

The Christian walk is not an easy life on the surface. The Word of God says that we will be hated in all the world for Christ namesake (Matt. 24:9). The Bible says that in the last days are enemy prevail against us physically until Christ returns to save us (Dan 7:21, 22). Furthermore, we must endure hardship as a good soldier of Jesus Christ (2 Tim 2:3) and yet we are never alone in this, God promises us that He will never leave us nor forsake us if we believe in him (Matt.28:20).

In everything we go through we have the peace and joy of God which surpasses all understanding (Philp. 4:6-8) The Bible declares, "For I consider the sufferings of this present time are not worthy to be compared with the glory which shall be revealed in us". (Rom 8:18). However, in all these things we are more than conquerors through Jesus Christ (Rom. 8:37)

Stay In Contact

Our Contact Information

Stay in Contact with the American Christian Defense Alliance, Inc. though Our Website At: www.ACDAInc.Org

Join Our Mailing List

We also Greatly Appreciate You Signing Up For Our Mailing List and Providing a Good Rating and Review for this Book. Your Reviews help other people like yourself find this book and benefit from its contents.

If You or Your Family have been Blessed by this book please let us know by dropping us a line through our website at
http://acdainc.org

Thanks Again for Reading

God Bless!

Find All Our Books

Our Books:

Get the Entire 7 Book Series of Bible Studies for Belts

Martial Arts Ministry: How To Start A Martial Arts Ministry

Prayer: Your No. 1 Prayer Book To Learn To Be A Strong Christian Prayer Warrior That Prays With Powerful Prayers In The War Room To Overcome And Defeat The Enemy

Real Men Don't Make Promises: Understanding Oaths, Pacts, Covenants & Promises From A Biblical Perspective

A Vague Notion: How To Overcome Limiting Beliefs of Fear and Anxiety Through the Word of God

Biblical Bug Out: Don't Bug In - Follow The Calling

Christian Prepping 101: How To Start Prepping

Prepping: A Christian Perspective

Prepping: Survival Basics

Bug Out: Prepper Preparations for Survival, SHTF, Natural Disasters, Off Grid Living, Civil Unrest, and Martial Law to Help You Survive the End Times

Overcoming 50 Shades of Grey And All The Colors Of The LGBT Rainbow: How To Conquer Your Lust and Walk In The Spirit Of God

Salvation for Your Unsaved Mom: 10 Things to Tell Your Mom Before She Dies

Parenting: How To Be A Great Parent And Raise Awesome Kids

How To Finance Your Full-Time RV Dream

Biblical Bug Out: Don't Bug In - Follow the Calling

BY: TOM ECKERD

Copyright © 2016

American Christian Defense Alliance, Inc.

Baltimore, Maryland

ACDAInc.Org

All Rights Reserved. No part of this publication may be reproduced in any form or by any means, including scanning, photocopying, or otherwise without prior written permission of the copyright holder.

Special Request

Thank you for purchasing our book and supporting our Ministry. We actually have two requests – To Pray for Our Ministry and to Read this Book All the Way through. No Ministry can survive without Prayer and Support so we ask you to keep our Ministry in Your Daily Prayers and Pray as the Lord leads.

We encourage you to Read the Book you purchased all the way through. Many Books NEVER Get Read, and the ones that do only get read the first few pages.

One of our Special Request is that if you are serious about learning the material in this book that you take time to actually read this book in its entirety – all the way through.

We all lead such busy lives nowadays and can get side tracked so easily please take a moment to consider my words and read to the end of the book and keep us in Your Prayers.

Thank You once again for purchase. We deeply appreciate Your Prayers and Support and know that God will Bless You as You continue to Bless this Ministry.

Dedication

This Book is dedicated to All the Christian Patriots Out there who continue to stand in the Gap, Standing up for the Word of God and the Testimony of Our Lord Jesus Christ - Pressing on, Enduring, Persevering evermore closer to Your reward in Heaven.

Knowing that time is short, Understanding it goes way beyond National Boundaries – For Our Kingdom is Not of this World – Yet!

Stand Fast in the Knowledge of the Truth My Brothers & Sisters and Continue to "Take Action for the Kingdom of God" in real and practical ways being sensitive always to the leading and guiding of the Holy Spirit.

Forward

So many so-called Christians (which are not actually Christians) live a life void of understanding the times we live in and the hardship that awaits anyone who truly follows Christ. Regardless of specific dates or doctrines we know for certain that persecution is on the rise throughout the world for Christians. We all must be ready for the day that our lives are shattered with the reality of being "hated in all the world". Being merely hated is one thing, but as any reasonable person can conclude – what happens after they hate us? The obvious answer is they will come for us just like they have come for the Jews in WWII.

This book is an attempt to help guide the people that God calls to read this book onto the proper path of Bugging Out and not staying put in their homes and becoming a victim of the time to come.

This book is but the first in a series to come to help educate and prepare the Saints of God with the Word of God regarding the times we live in and how God wants His people to respond to such matters. I hope you will join with us in spreading this message as time is of the essence – We must all act with a sense of urgency, compassion, and love.

The Time Is Now!

Chapter 1:
Is Bugging Out Really God's Plan?

Prepping doesn't give us one universal answer which works for everyone and every situation. Each individual's case is different, as well as their needs. For followers of Christ, prepping raises some questions that have to be answered; some of which are quite difficult, such as the whole question of whether or not we should be prepping in the first place. We are commanded to operate in faith and some see prepping as operating in fear, rather than faith.

Another area of question is the concept of bugging out. Once again, this can be broken down into a faith versus fear question by some, especially those who are against the idea of bugging out. Yet, before we rashly answer that question, we must search the scriptures and see what they say. Are there biblical examples of bugging out? If so, are there specific contexts which dictate that bugging out is the correct course of action?

The truth is, we find many examples of bugging out in scripture, starting in Genesis and running through much of the Bible. While not all of the movement of God's people from place to place can be attributed to bugging out, there are sufficient examples for us to use, in order to establish it as a biblical principle.

Our earliest example of a bug out was Jacob in Genesis, chapter 27 and 28. While this isn't the best example of a bug out or even the best example of a reason for a bug out, it still stands as the earliest. Jacob had a personal problem in his life, which he had brought upon himself. He stole his brother's blessing and was in fear for his life. This worried his mother, Rebekah, who counseled him to flee to her brother, Laban, in Haran. Jacob obeys, fleeing from his brother, before his brother could kill him.

A much better example of a bug out occurs near the end of Genesis. This is the largely ignored part of the story of Joseph's life.

Everyone concentrates on Joseph, how he was sold into slavery by his brothers and how he was raised up to be Pharaoh's right hand man. But few talk about God's purpose behind all this and the bug out his family made to get away from the drought.

There was drought and famine in the land of Canaan, where Jacob and his sons lived. Twice, the sons traveled to Egypt, purchasing grain from Joseph, the brother they had sold into slavery; but Joseph tried to hide his identity from them, even playing tricks on them. Finally, on the second trip, after arresting them for the supposed crime of stealing his silver cup, Joseph breaks down and cries, revealing himself to them. He then invites them to move to Egypt, where he takes care of them through the drought. In chapter 46, Jacob and his family bug out from Canaan and go to Egypt.

This example clearly fits our understanding of a bug out, as it was caused by a natural disaster. Jacob and his sons went to Egypt for the explicit purpose of avoiding a drought and the resulting famine.

A little over 400 years later, we find that the Israelites were still living in Egypt. By then, they had become a mighty people, so numerous that the Egyptians were afraid of them. In reaction to that fear, the Egyptians enslaved them, putting them to work building Pharaoh's cities.

Yet the fear did not go away. The Israelites continued to prosper and grow, which enraged their erstwhile masters and caused them to mistreat the Israelites even more, even commanding the midwives to kill all baby boys. Of course, those midwives were Israelites themselves, so they didn't obey that command. But something had to be done; it was time for another bug out.

This time, the bug out was predicated on government oppression, rather than a natural disaster; but it was still a bug out. The Israelites called out to God and asked His help. He provided it through a man named Moses, an unusual man, who although he had been raised in Pharaoh's palace, was of the people of Israel.

Herein we find an important lesson for ourselves. Bugging out doesn't preclude faith nor does it mean that we've abandoned faith. Rather, it should be done as an act of faith and in conjunction with God's guidance and provision. To bug out without God would be foolish, as we would be leaving behind our greatest survival asset.

The Israelites were successful in their bug out and spent the next 40 years living off the land, as God gave them provision. Finally, they came to their new homeland, the same one which Jacob had fled over 400 years earlier.

About 450 years later, we find another example of a personal bug out, that of King David. His third son, Absalom, decided that he was destined to be king and rose up in rebellion against his father. Being an astute man, he plotted carefully, gaining the support of the people before taking any overt action. Thus, by the time David came to understand what was happening, he was in danger and fled Jerusalem.

This was a personal bug out, although David took much of his family and royal court with him. Rather than bugging out to avoid a natural disaster or to flee persecution under an unjust government, he fled to save his life. In a sense, we can equate that to a bug out that is undertaken to get away from marauding gangs that want to break into your home during a time of social unrest and lawlessness; for that was the situation that Absalom created and which David fled.

David was away from Jerusalem for several months, moving from place to place in a constant escape and evasion action, hiding from his son. Finally, the general of his army, Joab, killed Absalom, in direct violation of David's command. Nevertheless, it was once again safe and David could return to his palace in Jerusalem.

"Yes, you might be saying, but these are all Old Testament events, what about New Testament examples of bug outs, do they exist as well?"

I'm glad you asked. We don't have as many examples in the New Testament, because the history of the New Testament covers a much shorter time period, but we do have examples. The first of these is when Joseph and Mary fled Judah and went to Egypt, because Herod wanted to kill the newborn king, Jesus.

Once again, we see God Himself involved in bugging out. An angel of the Lord spoke to Joseph in a dream, in Matthew 2:13, telling him to flee to Egypt, in order to protect Jesus from death. They did, living in Egypt for several years, until Herod died and it was safe to return. In that case, we could say that God also arranged provision, just as He did for the Israelites in the desert. The gifts of the Magi; gold, frankincense and myrrh were valuable gifts, which when sold would provide them with many years of provision.

We also find the early church bugging out, in order to avoid persecution. Acts 8:1 tells us:

> *And at that time there was a great persecution against the church which was at Jerusalem; and they were all scattered abroad throughout the regions of Judea and Samaria, except the apostles. [2] And devout men carried Stephen to his burial, and made great lamentation over him. [3] As for Saul, he made havoc of the church, entering into every house, and haling men and women committed them to prison. [4] Therefore they that were scattered abroad went everywhere preaching the word.*

This began the spreading of the Gospel throughout the world, completing the Great Commission. Had it not been for the early persecution of the church, that commandment may never have been fulfilled. But as with all things, God used it to complete His plans.

So we see bugging out as both an Old Testament and a New Testament principle, carried out by God's people as needed. We also see that God's people depended on his help and his guidance to bug out, in order that they might accomplish His will.

Chapter 2:
Why God Called Us to Bug Out?

We saw clearly in chapter one that there are times when God not only allows His people to bug out, but actually calls them to do so. Since God never changes, but is the same yesterday, today and forever (Heb 13:8), we can safely assume the He will continue to work in the same way in our lives, that He worked in the lives of these people whom we find mentioned in the Bible.

But that begs the question of "Why?" Why would God want people to bug out? There has to be a purpose, as everything God does is for some divine purpose. It may not be readily obvious to us, but that doesn't mean that there is no purpose, merely demonstrates that God's ways are higher than ours (Isa 55:9), making them at times, hard for us to understand.

The book of Esther in the Old Testament is an interesting story. Once again, it is a story that we largely ignore, allowing it to serve as something to be told to children, while we occupy ourselves with the more important things of the New Testament. Yet, if it had not been for the events of that book, we could not be saved.

We tend to think the story is about Esther, as she is the main actor in it. But in fact, Esther is nothing more than a tool in God's hand. He chose her in His infinite wisdom, for such a time, knowing that Satan was going to try to destroy His people, the Jews. The story is about how God used Esther to thwart Satan's plans.

That was clearly not a bug out situation, but it demonstrates to us how critical God's plans are. Since Jesus was prophesied to be a descendant of King David, it was essential that David's bloodline survive. But if Satan's plans had been fulfilled in the book of Esther, David's bloodline, along with all of the other descendants of Abraham, Isaac and Jacob would have been destroyed.

That would have made God's prophecy a lie and with it negated the work of the cross.

Maybe you and I don't have such an important place in God's ultimate plans; but we can know without a doubt that we have some place. He has called us and saved us for a purpose beyond our own salvation. Even if that is nothing more than to lead one other person to Him, that is an important purposes.

When we look at end time prophecy, we see calamity coming to Earth. While most Christians believe that we won't be here for those events, we truly don't know. Scripture is not clear on the exact timing of the rapture. But even if it was, Jesus Himself referred to a time He called "the beginning of sorrows" (Matt 24:8) in which there will be wars, famine, pestilences and earthquakes. That's before the events of the Great Tribulation and quite probably before the rapture. In that case, we may need to bug out, in order to avoid those disasters.

To back this up, Jesus told us to be ready to flee. In Luke 17:30-33, He said:

> *Even thus shall it be in the day when the Son of man is revealed. [31] In that day, he which shall be upon the housetop, and his stuff in the house, let him not come down to take it away: and he that is in the field, let him likewise not return back. [32] Remember Lot's wife. [33] Whosoever shall seek to save his life shall lose it; and whosoever shall lose his life shall preserve it.*

We must note that this verse ties in directly with those talking about the beginning of sorrows in Matthew, chapter 24. This is no accident. In both cases, Jesus was talking about end times events. Therefore, we can be sure that there will come a day when we, the Body of Christ, will need to bug out. It will happen shortly before the rapture and it would be best if we were prepared.

Chapter 3:
Spiritual Awareness

The big question the church has faced, throughout its history, is when the Lord will return. Countless dates have been picked by one minister or another, as the date for the coming of the Lord, and yet He tarries. The truth is, we have no idea of when he will return, just the promise that He will.

> *But of that day and hour knoweth no man, no, not the angels of heaven, but my Father only.*
>
> *- Matthew 24:36*

There are many signs given in scripture, talking about when the Lord will return; but as with many things in prophecy, they are not clear. It is easy to misinterpret prophecy, seeing things that we want to see, in what is going on around us. This is nothing new, as even the Disciples of Christ misunderstood His coming and His purpose in being here.

The book of Acts opens with the last time Jesus is with His disciples, before being taken up to heaven. He had already spent over three years with them, teaching them and ministering with them. Even more than that, He had died and been raised from the dead. Yet they were still misunderstanding His message. They asked Him in verse 6, *"Lord, wilt thou at this time restore again the kingdom to Israel?"*

We could speak badly of the disciples for their lack of discernment, but that wouldn't be fair. I seriously doubt that any of us would do much better. It is much easier to misinterpret prophecy than it is to interpret it correctly.

But I don't really believe that God expects us to interpret it... at least not before the fact. He tells us in Isaiah 48 that the purpose of prophecy is so that once he does something, we know that it was Him. That's after the fact, not before.

I have declared the former things from the beginning; and they went forth out of my mouth, and I showed them; I did them suddenly, and they came to pass. [4] *Because I knew that thou art obstinate, and thy neck is an iron sinew, and thy brow brass;* [5] *I have even from the beginning declared it to thee; before it came to pass I showed it thee: lest thou shouldest say, Mine idol hath done them, and my graven image, and my molten image, hath commanded them.*

- Isaiah 48:3-5

Since we don't know when He is coming, we must live as if it will happen any minute. At the same time, we must be prepared to stay here, doing the Lord's work, till the end of our lives. We can't abandon one for the other and still fulfill all that we have been called to do.

But not everything that may cause a need to bug out is associated with the end times.

The examples we looked at earlier weren't dealing with end time events, but rather with things that were going on in people's lives; whether from natural disasters or disastrous rulers. Either way, they needed to bug out in order to survive. The same can happen to us at any time.

The inhabitants of New Orleans needed to bug out in 2005, but many didn't. Because they didn't, over 1,000 of them died in Hurricane Katrina. Had they been more discerning, they would have followed the government mandate to evacuate the city and bugged out, saving their lives.

Natural disasters can happen at any time. There is literally no part of the country which is immune to them. Not all parts are susceptible to hurricanes, but those that aren't are susceptible to other forms of natural disaster. Each requires preparation and many give us valid reason to bug out and avoid being caught in the disaster.

But there are much more serious things happening in our world today; things that could affect the whole nation. While it is possible to point to many different things, I want to mention just two. I mention these, because of all the man-made disasters that could befall us, these two are the most likely.

The first is a financial collapse. Our country's economy is still reeling from the effects of the 2008-2009 housing crash. Regardless of the numbers that the Obama administration is putting out, there are more people out of work today, then there were when he entered office. The number they are reporting is bogus, because they only look at those who are receiving unemployment compensation; but the labor participation rate, the number of people who are actually working, is still going down.

On top of that, most of the "new jobs" which have been created in the last seven years are part-time jobs, rather than full-time ones. That means we have a few million people in the population, who are working part-time, when they need full-time work.

We can thank Obamacare for that, as businesses can't afford to hire full-time employees and are trying to hire part-time whenever they can. With the IRS determination that "full-time work" is 30 hours or more per week, those companies are only allowing people to work 25 hours.

The other high risk we are facing is that of an EMP attack. While there are several ways of creating an EMP, the one that holds the highest risk is that of exploding a nuclear device above the atmosphere. If that happens, then the full force of the explosion leaves the bomb as electromagnetic energy. That energy strips electrons from the molecules in the upper atmosphere, amplifying its effect.

When those electrons reach the surface of the earth, they act like an extremely powerful radio wave, causing a spike that is 100 times greater than lightning. That spike will destroy pretty much all solid-state electronics, as well as destroying the electrical grid.

According to the report by the EMP commission, such an attack would have the net effect of sending this country back to the mid-1800s. About 90% of the population would die due to starvation or sickness. Our country would be destroyed and people would be fighting over the table scraps, trying to survive.

Either of these situations could cause a breakdown of society, including a breakdown of law and order. If there is any one time that a bug out is appropriate, that's it. Bugging in at such a time would all but guarantee your home being attacked, especially if people got the idea that you had a stockpile of food. It would be much safer to bug out, giving your family a much greater chance of survival, than to bug in.

The thing is, we're not likely to receive much of a notice of these events happening... at least, not in the natural. But God always takes care of His people. Over and over again, we see in the Bible how God warns his people of things to come. If we are sensitive to the voice of his Holy Spirit, that still small voice that Elijah heard in the cave (1 Kings 19:2), we will receive the necessary warning of what is to come. When that happens, we must be ready to flee.

Chapter 4:
How to Start Your Bug-Out Preparations

Before you start doing anything, you need to make sure your head is in the right place. As believers in Jesus Christ, everything we do must come out of faith, not fear. Why is that? Because when we walk in fear, we allow the devil to have control of our lives, but when we walk in faith, we put God in control.

This idea of walking in faith is so important, that Paul told the Romans that anything they did, without faith, was actually sin:

> *And he that doubteth is damned if he eat, because he eateth not of faith: for <u>whatsoever is not of faith is sin</u>.*
>
> *Romans 14:23*

One could easily ignore that verse, because it is in the midst of a trestle about eating food offered to idols. The verse itself talks about that as well. Since that isn't part of our culture, we might think it doesn't apply. But the important part is the last seven words, "whatsoever is not of faith is sin." This can be seen as the opposite side of Hebrews 11:6:

> *But without faith it is impossible to please him: for he that cometh to God must believe that he is, and that he is a rewarder of them that diligently seek him.*
>
> *Hebrews 11:6*

So the first and most important part of our preparation has to be getting our thoughts in order. We must *"Cast down imaginations and every high thing that exalteth itself against the knowledge of God..."* (2 Cor 10:5). While there are many things which we could talk about which could fall into this category of "imaginations" or "high things," there is one which I am sure qualifies, that is fear.

Praise God that we don't have any reason why we need to operate in fear. While we have the capacity for fear, we are not committed to it in any way. Any fear that we have, did not come from God.

> *For God hath not given us the spirit of fear; but of power, and of love, and of a sound mind.*
>
> *2 Timothy 1:7*

Okay, so it's clear that we should not be preparing for a crisis situation because of fear. Does that mean we should ignore those situations altogether? No; we should prepare out of love, specifically a love for our families and a desire to take care of them. God has entrusted them to us, and while we depend on Him for provision and all our needs, we are not called to just sit on the sofa and watch television. We are called to work and prepare.

One of the really great things about preparing out of love for our families, is that it helps to protect us from fear. Love and fear are incompatible. When one is in operation, it prevents the other from working:

> *There is no fear in love; <u>but perfect love casteth out fear</u>: because fear hath torment. He that feareth is not made perfect in love.*
>
> 1 John 4:18

So get your love going. Take action based on that. As long as you keep yourself operating in love, you won't be operating in fear. Your love and your focus on that love will protect you from fear entering in and taking control of you.

That's all fine and dandy, but what's the first step?

As in many things, the first step is knowledge. You've got to have an idea of what it is that you need to do, before you can take action and do it; otherwise, all you're going to do is waste a lot of time and money. Fortunately for you, you've taken the first step. Buying this book is setting you on the road towards preparedness.

Of course, you need to take action on the things you learn from this book. Preparedness is not just a mindset (although that is an important part of it), but a whole series of actions. Your actions will determine how prepared you are and how well you are able to do, once a true disaster strikes.

Don't let your learning stop here either. This book will help you prepare to bug out, when that time comes, but it doesn't discuss how to survive in the wilderness. You need to learn a whole new set of skills, so that you are ready to survive and keep your family alive, when the time comes to bug out and go to the mountains.

Chapter 5:
Where Do I Go?

Any bug out requires a destination. If you don't have any idea of where you are going, then all you are doing is running away. While there are times when that may be necessary, that isn't the way to ensure your survival. You need an integrated plan, which includes where you are going, how you're going to get there and what you'll do to survive in your bug out retreat.

Fortunately, the Bible gives us some guidance on this. It says,

> *Then let them which are in Judea <u>flee to the mountains</u>; and let them which are in the midst of it depart out; and let not them that are in the countries enter thereinto.*
>
> *Luke 21:21*

Essentially the same guidance is given to us in Mark 13:14, with the difference being that it specifically mentions the *"abomination of desolation, spoken of by Daniel..."* Of course, the problem with that is that we are not likely to recognize that abomination when it comes. So, we can choose to ignore that advice, assuming that whatever disaster is happening isn't the abomination, or we can choose to follow that advice, assuming that the disaster we are experiencing is the abomination of desolation. Personally, I prefer the second option, as it carries the greater security for my family.

But the real point I want to bring out here is the one about where we are to flee to. Jesus Himself gave some very specific instructions on that; He said to *"flee to the mountains."* Now, I don't really know why Jesus said that or why He chose the mountains. But as an expert on survival, I can say that He made the best possible choice. But then, He knows everything, so that's not a surprise.

The thing is, there really is no better place to try and survive than in the mountains. Survival requires that you have the necessary resources. While you will be bringing some of those with you, and we'll talk later about caching some supplies for you to use, there's no way that you can take enough supplies to last you the rest of your life. You're going to need to learn to live off the land.

Living off the land is challenging. But living off the land in the mountains, where you are surrounded by forests, game and fish is much easier than trying to survive in the middle of a Kansas cornfield. Everything you need is there, more so than anywhere else. Specifically, the mountains provide:

    Forests to hide in
    Wood for fire
    Building materials (trees and rocks)
    Animals to eat
    Fish to eat
    Edible plants
    Sources of water

Not only that, but the mountains will do a better job of hiding you from prying eyes than anywhere else. Sounds are deceptive in the mountains, with echoes and sounds bouncing down canyons. Even if you use a firearm to shoot game, someone looking for you would have a hard time to pinpoint exactly where you were. The short line-of-sight helps too, as it's difficult to look over broad areas, searching for a particular person or target.

Now, the Lord doesn't give us guidance as to which mountain we should bug out to; that's up to you and me. But don't wait until it's time to bug out, in order to select the mountain. You want to have a specific destination in mind; someplace you can get to in a reasonable amount of time, where you will have everything you need.

Ideally, you would be best off if you owned a cabin in the mountains and could stockpile supplies there.

That way, when you bug out, you have some place to go, that's ready and prepared for you. But few of us can afford that. You'll probably have to find a spot to go to and plan on building a shelter when you get there.

Joel Skousen has a wonderful book that can help you find someplace that would work as a bug out location. It's his book, "Strategic Relocation" the third edition. This new edition adds a whole lot of new material and new areas to what he had before. If you don't know where to go, I'd highly recommend it.

Chapter 6: How Do I Get There?

Most people think of driving when they think of bugging out. Some even go so far as to invest in massive four-wheel-drive trucks, just for that purpose. That's not surprising though, considering that we are highly mobile society, which is used to taking a car wherever we go.

There's just one problem with that idea. If you're bugging out, there's a good chance that a whole lot of other people are going to be bugging out at the same time. That means that the roads will be crowded with people who are unprepared. They'll run out of gas and their cars will overheat, turning the highways into parking lots.

If you have a 4x4 truck or SUV, you might be able to go around the traffic, heading out across country. A lot will depend on where you live and what sorts of fields you will have to pass through. If you live in the middle of Texas ranchlands, there will probably be dirt trails you can take across country.

But if you live in the middle of New Jersey, you're not going to find that. So, before spending money on that truck, take a look at your route and determine whether it will help you or not.

You need to plan your route in detail, looking at road conditions, probable traffic problems and alternate routes you can take. As much as possible, find the back way to get there, preferably a back way that few others will know about. Avoid major highways, roads, intersections and bridges as much as possible.

If your route involves a highway, then know where you can get off that highway and take an alternate route. I'm not just talking about places where there are side roads either. Can you take out across some farmer's pasture? How about some power line right-of-way? Don't limit your thinking to roads, think in terms of places you can get through with a vehicle, a pony cart or on foot.

Chances are, you're not going to be able to get where you're going in a car; maybe not even in a 4x4 truck. However, that's not to say that you shouldn't have plans to bug out in your vehicle; just that you shouldn't be wedded to that idea. Go as far as you can in the vehicle, but be ready to abandon it at any time and continue on foot, man's oldest means of transportation.

Traveling on foot is difficult and slow. When the wagon trains were going west, they averaged ten miles per day. In some types of terrain, travel was so slow that when they stopped at night, they could still see the place they had camped the night before.

If your family is in good shape and your children are somewhat grown up, you might be able to make ten miles per day, walking. But if you're traveling with small children, don't expect to make more than three or four miles per day. A push cart can help with this, as you can put the children in it and push them along, saving time.

For that matter, a push cart can also be a way of increasing how much you can carry. Your bug out bag is limited to 40 or 50 pounds.

But if you can use a cart, you can add another 100 pounds of food and supplies. That's well worth considering. Just make sure it has large enough wheels for the terrain you'll have to cross.

As you travel, you'll need to stay alert about everything that is going on around you. As some people say it, "Keep your head on a swivel." That way, you can see behind you, as well as in front. There will be others traveling as well, and the most dangerous predator on the face of the Earth is the two-legged one. You have to assume that anyone else you see is going to be a hostile and want to take what you have.

There are a lot of people who think that the law will be thrown out the window in a bug out situation. That's a dangerous way to think. Basically, it's the way the bad guys think. But even if there is a breakdown of society with a breakdown of law and order, the rule of law will eventually be reestablished. When that happens, they will investigate anyone who found it necessary to kill someone else, even in self-defense.

Ideally, you want to avoid those confrontations. But if you have one, keep in mind that the law will still apply, even if there is nobody there to arrest you. The technical terminology is that it's legal to use deadly force for self-defense or the defense of others, as long you are in imminent danger of life or limb. Your defense of your actions has to be able to pass the test of reasonableness. That means a reasonable person taking reasonable action in the circumstances. If you can't demonstrate that, you could be charged with murder.

Chapter 7:
What to Do When I Get There?

Living in the wild is a complicated and difficult task; you've got to get pretty much everything you need directly from nature herself. In this, you need to understand your priorities and make sure that you work in alignment with those priorities. Failure to take care of everything in a meaningful, logical way could prove to be fatal, especially when you find that you don't have something critical that you need.

But before you start with any of your normal survival priorities, you've got to keep yourself alive. That means keeping yourself alive from the two-legged predators and anyone else who might be looking for you. If things are dangerous enough that you've decided you have to bug out, then I think it's safe to say that they are dangerous everywhere.

You'll want to do everything you can to stay out of people's sight as you are approaching your bug out retreat. The last thing you will want to do is lead them right to where you're planning on hiding out. So take the time to check your back trail carefully, looking for others who may be on it. Watch for the smoke from their campfires, look for colors that don't belong, listen for noise that doesn't come from nature and look for the flash of light from anything, as that's probably them.

High points are an excellent place for doing this surveillance along your back trail. When you stop at night and again before you leave in the morning, take a look from a high point. If you cross a ridge, stop there are do it as well.

When you are getting close to your destination, take a deceptive path, as if you are going around it or you are going to pass it. If you can, walk in the water for a ways, so that you don't leave a path. When you come out of the water, do so on rock, so that here are no tracks for anyone to follow. Walk on rock whenever you can. If necessary use deadfalls, but rock is better.

Upon arrival at your bug out retreat, your first action must be to establish your perimeter security. Use the people you have at your disposal, your family or survival team, and keep some on guard at all times. Patrol the area, looking for bad guys or any sign of them passing near. Do everything you can to avoid leaving sign of your own. That means to walk without leaving tracks, breaking sticks or leaving threads from your clothes hanging from a bush.

Of course, you're going to have to integrate your self-defense tasks with your other survival tasks. It won't do you the least bit of good to protect yourself from dying in one way, only to succumb in some other. While those two-legged predators are dangerous, the biggest killer in the wild is hypothermia.

There are certain priorities which are essential to survival. You've got to make sure you meet those needs, or you're just not going to make it. The top priorities are normally referred to as the rule of 3s:

> You can die of loss of body heat in 30 minutes
> You can die of lack of water in 3 days
> You can die of lack of food in 30 days

So, start by keeping yourself warm. That means setting up a shelter and starting a fire. You want to be careful with your fire, because a visible fire can be seen for miles at night. Likewise, smoke can be seen for miles in the daytime. So, you need to make sure that your fire is hidden by a stone fire pit and located under a tree, allowing the tree's branches to help dissipate the smoke. Use only dry wood, as it will smoke much less than damp wood will.

Your shelter must be hidden as well, regardless of what kind it is. Before building it, look around the area and pick somewhere that it will be hidden.

A building in the middle of a mountain valley makes it rather obvious that someone is living there. Better to hide it in the middle of the forest and plant brush and saplings all around it to hide it. Use camouflage as much as possible for your shelter and for everything you do.

The idea is to blend into your surroundings and become invisible. The better you can do that, the less likely you are to be found. At the same time, you'll need to be active, hauling water, hunting for food, gathering plants and firewood, maybe even tending a vegetable garden. All that activity makes you vulnerable to being seen and attacked.

You can do a lot to hide yourself and your activities. Lean to move through the underbrush without leaving a trail or making noise. Moccasins are much better for this than boots, as they don't have a distinct edge like a shoe or boot sole does. But in order to have moccasins, you'll need to kill an animal and tan the hide.

Avoid using the same path over and over or you'll leave a visible trail to follow. When you get water, approach the water from a different direction every time. That way, you can't be ambushed as easily. Vary your routine and you'll make it more difficult for the bad guys.

Of course, you've got to stay armed at all times. Make your guns part of you. Your handgun should be on your person from the time you wake up till the time you go to bed. Whenever you leave your shelter, you should take your long gun or bow with you. That includes going 50 feet to get some water.

Your days living in the wild will be busy ones. There will be plenty for you to do, in order to keep yourself and your family alive. Be sure to use your time wisely, so as to get everything done. At the same time, stay alert. As you learn the sounds and habits of the animals in the forest, they will warn you of anyone coming. That will become the best alarm system you could have, even better than what you can do yourself.

Chapter 8:
The Bug Out Bag

When the time comes to bug out, you're going to need equipment and supplies to survive; that's where the bug out bag comes in. You're not going to be able to go to someplace where you can pick up a loaf of bread and a gallon of milk at the corner store. Nor are you likely to find an abandoned cabin in the woods, with a welcome sign hanging on the door. You're going to have to live off of what you take with you, the knowledge you have and what nature provides.

So, it's best to take as much with you as possible, specifically the things that will help you survive out in the wild. Of course, that means knowing how to use those things to survive with as well. Ultimately, the most important thing you can take with you is the knowledge of how to survive.

The bug out bag must provide for all of your basic needs, so it would be a good idea to review what those are. In order of priority, your needs are:

    Oxygen
    Maintaining your body heat . . . .
    (This includes clothing, shelter and fire)
    Purified water
    Food
    Self-defense
    First-aid (including personal hygiene)

The one thing on that list that you can't take along with you is oxygen. Fortunately, we have that in the air all around us. If something happens where oxygen is no longer available, I'm afraid that survival will be beyond the purview of this book.

Carrying all of that is going to be a bit difficult. You have to assume that you're going to have to go on foot at some point.

Even if you leave home in your car or truck, chances are that you'll have to abandon it along the way. With that in mind, you need to make your bug out bag something that you can carry, such as a backpack. While other things can be used, a backpack is your best bet.

When selecting a backpack, try to avoid something that is obviously military in appearance. That's too easy to identify as what it is. You don't want people to realize that you're bugging out or recognize that you're prepared. So, you're better off with a backpacker's backpack, rather than a military one.

You want to make sure that whatever backpack you pick has a weight-bearing belt. Your legs are much stronger than your back, and can support the weight of the backpack and its contents easier than your back can. But if the pack doesn't have a belt, your back will have to carry the weight.

Most people have to limit their pack to about one-fourth their body weight. But that's assuming that you're in shape. If not, you'll have to make it even less. One way to compensate for this is to have every member of the family carry their own pack. While women and children can't carry as big or heavy a pack as a man can, they should be able to carry their own clothes, personal toiletries and sleeping bag, as well as some of the communal food.

Bug out bags are very personal, simply because each person's situation is unique. You need to match the pack you carry to your needs, the terrain you are going to travel through, the area you are going to set up camp and your own survival skills. There's absolutely no sense in carrying equipment you can't use, no matter how useful it might seem.

With that in mind, here's what you should include:

Shelter

> Backpacking tent (or make your own shelter from available materials)
> Tarp
> Cordage (paracord is best)
> Duct tape
> Wire ties (useful for tying branches together)
> Backpacking sleeping bag (or blanket) (each person)

Clothing (each person)

> One set of rugged, warm clothing
> Extra socks
> Coat (seasonally appropriate)
> Hat (also seasonally appropriate)
> Work gloves
> Rain poncho

Fire

Fire starters (at least two primary - waterproof matches and a disposable lighter; and one secondary - BlastMatch, Metal Match or Ferro Rod)

Fire accelerant (WetFire cubes are excellent, or you can make your own by working petroleum jelly into cotton balls)

Purified water

Canteen or water bottle (minimum 1 liter, two are better than one) (each person)

Water purifying straw (Lifestraw is best) (each person)

Bag-type water filter (one for the family)

WAPI - water pasteurization indicator (one for the family)

Food

Enough food to last for five days (dried foods are best, lightest weight)
Survival fishing kit
Wire for snares
Backpacking cookware set (each person)
Backpacking cups and plates (each person)
Backpacking utensils (each person)
Camp stove (not essential, but can be useful)

Self-defense

Firearms (each person who can shoot should have a pistol and a long gun)
Extra ammo (caution, ammo is heavy)
Bow (also good for hunting)
Additional weapons (if you have family members skilled in their use)

First-aid

Trauma first-aid kit (this is bigger than your typical family first-aid kit and designed for dealing with larger injuries
Personal hygiene needs
Anti-bacterial hand cleaner (great when you don't have water available)

Tools

Camp hatchet (preferably with a built-in hammer)
Folding pruning saw (for cutting wood)
Folding saw
Sheath knife (each person)
Multi-tool (useful for multiple things)
Tactical flashlight (each person, with extra batteries)

As you can see, this list is rather lengthy; but unless you are going to make everything yourself, once you get there, you really need it all. Keep weight in mind on all your purchases.

When looking at things like backpacking tents and cookware, you're really paying for weight savings. The lighter it is, the more expensive it is. Don't skimp on quality, as your life and that of your family is riding on that equipment performing as it should.

Try to buy items which are multi-purpose whenever you can. That's a good way to save weight. There's an axiom in the prepping community, which has been stolen from the military. It goes, "Two is one and one is none." That speaks of the need for redundancy. If something breaks or becomes lost, you'll need something you can fall back on.

Chapter 9:
Creating Supply Caches

There's no way that anyone can carry all the supplies they'll need for a prolonged stay in the wilderness. A typical bug out bag only has three days of rations in it. If you do it like I do, then you'll have five days worth. But even that's not enough, and you really can't carry more. Weight limitations are going to control how much you can fit in your pack.

Now, if you're Grizzly Adams, that won't be a problem, because you'll just be able to live off the land. But then, Adams lived a few hundred years ago, when there were many fewer people in this country and much more wild game. The prairies are no longer covered with buffalo as far as the eye can see and even deer, which are by no means nearing extinction are not as plentiful as they once were.

So, you're going to have to have supplies to live off of, especially food. While you will probably be able to augment your food supplies somewhat from nature, you can't really count on that too much, especially at the beginning. There's no way you can count on it for the majority of your needs. Since you can't carry it and you can't hunt for it, you're going to have to get food from other people. That means, buying it ahead of time and creating caches of food that you can access when the time comes.

Notice that I say "caches" and not "cache." You really don't just want one cache. There are several problems with having only one cache, top amongst them being that others could find it and you could lose everything.

Side Note – If you're enjoying this book why not stop by our website and check us out at www.acdainc.org.

Any cache needs to contain an assortment of your most critical supplies. That mostly means food, but should also include:

- Toilet paper
- Personal hygiene supplies
- Medical supplies
- Fishing supplies
- Ammunition
- Matches
- Vegetable seeds

The food in your caches should be lightweight, high energy, with about a 20 percent protein content. If you are bugging out into an area where game and fish will be plentiful, you can lower the protein content a bit; but make sure you have some. For high energy, concentrate on carbohydrates, which your body can break down into simple sugars to provide energy.

You may also want to consider adding clothing to your caches, especially if you have growing children. You'll need clothes for them, when they outgrow the ones they'll be wearing when you bug out.

A five gallon plastic bucket makes a great cache, as it can be filled, sealed and buried, without any risk of the contents being destroyed by moisture, animals or insects. The bucket itself will be useful as well for a variety of tasks around your survival retreat. If you need more space, you can use multiple buckets or you can use 55 gallon drums. The only problem with the drums is finding ones with removable lids.

Your best bet is to bury your caches in the wilderness. Make a ring of them a few hours walk around your expected bug out location, so that you can reach them fairly easily. Place some along the route as well, so that you have some source of resupply while you are traveling. If you have to travel on foot to reach your bug out location, you'll need resupply before you can get there.

The hardest part of this is remembering where you left your cache. If you are burying them, they will be extremely hard to find. Make sure you pick good landmarks, which won't change.

Many people pick trees, but those are some of the worst landmarks you can pick. Trees can be destroyed by forest fire, killed by disease or cut down by other people. Better to pick things like rock outcroppings, which won't change with time.

Another option is to rent a storage space in a rural town that is nearby your bug out location. This could be a larger cache, but by no means should be your only one. The advantage here is that it doesn't have to be buried. But depending on the reason for your bug out, you may not be able to access it.

Keep in mind that you will never be able to retrieve everything that you have in your caches. Things will happen. Some sites will be destroyed by construction or nature herself. You'll lose your ability to find others. Events may keep you from going to even others. So, you ultimately want to have more caches than you'll need. That way, you can be sure of having enough.

Chapter 10:
Financial Considerations

It is possible to spend thousands of dollars trying to get ready for a disaster. I have seen people whose preparations have topped $10,000 and they're still working on more. Other families have moved their families to new areas, bugging out and getting off the grid before anything can happen. I'd hate to think what they are spending, but I'm sure it's more than ten grand.

Clearly, you can spend a lot of money preparing for a disaster. But that doesn't mean that you have to spend a lot of money. Actually, the more you know of survival skills, the less you need to spend. People without those skills have to spend the money, because they can't survive without all those fancy survival gadgets.

Learning survival skills is a good investment of your time. Not only will it save you money, but it will increase your family's chances of making it through, unscathed, if a disaster ever happens. Knowing what to do is at least 80 percent of the battle and having the stuff to do it with is the other 20 percent.

But for you and I, there is one other factor, which is more important; the Lord. More than anything, we need to be counting on the Lord to take care of us. Ultimately, it is His work, more than our own, which will help us to survive.

When the children of Israel were passing through the desert, God caused manna to fall upon the ground in the morning. He caused quail to descend on the camp in the evening. He had a rock which traveled with them and gave them water. God took care of their needs. Yes, they had to gather the manna and the quail, and they still had to cook it; but God made sure it was there.

God mandated that bug out, just as He has mandated our own. Well then, if He took care of the Israelites, why would we even entertain the thought that He wouldn't take care of us as well. We need to operate in faith, keeping our eyes fixed on Him.

Please note that the Israelites dependence on Jehovah God didn't preclude their leaving Egypt well prepared. Before they left, they were commanded to go to their neighbors, asking for gold and silver. They were told to take all their livestock with them (food). They went into the desert prepared to stay and never return. The largest bug out in history; and while they went prepared, they depended upon God for their true provision. That's a balance we need to emulate.

Our God is a God of provision. Everyone knows the verse, *"But my God shall supply all your need according to his riches in glory by Christ Jesus."* (Ph. 4:19). But knowing it and living it are two different things. We say we have faith in God, but when the rubber meets the road, we falter.

The thing is, in this sort of situation, you're going to have to depend on God for everything, or you aren't going to make it. That deer that wanders into camp so that you could kill it... God sent it. That rain that fell so that you could refill your water jugs... God sent that too. Yes, by all means, do your part; but in the larger part, depend on God and He will take care of you.

But for your and my part, we need to build our bug out bag and be ready to go. That raises the question, how much will that cost? If you look at some commercially available bug out bags on the market, you can easily spend two or three thousand dollars on them. But that doesn't mean you have to. My bug out bag, with the equipment in it that is included in the chapter on bug out bags, cost me less than $500, not counting weapons, a bow, my coat and fishing gear. I already had those things and the price on them can vary considerably.

I've seen bug out bags that people have made, which cost them less than $100, but I didn't choose to go that route. When you look over the list of equipment in my bag, you can see that it is heavy on survival gear. I could have gone cheaper, by not bringing as much. But I made the decision to go heavy on equipment, in order to increase my chances of survival.

The other expensive item to consider is your supply caches. Depending on how much you put in them and what you choose to put in them, those will probably cost you somewhere between $60 and $120 each. That price is for the ones in a 5-gallon bucket. Of course, a large cache will run more than that, perhaps several hundred dollars, once again, depending on what you put in them.

Chapter 11: Get Off the Grid

Most disasters bring with them a loss of electrical power. If the loss of power is severe enough and lasts long enough, it shuts down city water, communications and gas to homes as well. With that in mind, there's a lot of talk about going "off-grid" and either producing one's own electrical power or learning how to live without it. For most, the answer ends up being a combination between the two.

The problem with that is that our modern homes aren't designed for an off-grid lifestyle. If they were, we'd take advantage of solar power, passive solar heating, fuel efficient fireplaces or wood-burning stoves, root cellars and a host of other readily available technology, all designed to make off-grid living easier.

Okay, so what can we do? There are some people who are taking their off-grid living and moving out into the country; either to live in a cabin in the woods or to establish a true homestead.

But what if we took that concept a step further? What if we could create an off-grid lifestyle for ourselves, in a home that's truly designed to be self-contained and for living off the grid?

What I'm talking about here is the ultimate bug out. But I'm not just talking about it as something to do when things go to pot and you've got to abandon your home; I'm talking about doing it now; making it your new lifestyle. I'm talking about buying a RV, either a motorhome or a trailer and living in that.

If you were living in a RV, you could spend most of your time in places where you are already bugged out, away from the hustle and bustle of city life, as well as the dangers associated with being amongst a large number of people in the midst of social chaos. If a disaster happened, you wouldn't have to bug out, you'd already be bugged out.

Believe it or not, there are already a fair number of people who live like this; people you may not normally see.

Some are entertainers, working with circuses, carnivals and fairs. Others travel from trade-show to trade-show, selling their wares. Then there's probably the biggest group of all, retired people, who live in RVs so that they can travel and enjoy what's left of their lives. They go north in the summer, when it's nice up there and south in the winter to avoid the snow. They visit family and friends, taking their home with them. In between time, they stay at some campground, enjoying nature or the company of others who live the same lifestyle.

But you don't have to be retired in order to enjoy this sort of lifestyle. You can still work and be on the road at the same time, all you need is an internet connection that is reliable wherever you go.

More and more companies are hiring freelancers to take care of everything from engineering tasks to writing, accounting to graphic arts. If you have a skill that people need, you can find work through online agencies, connecting you with companies that will pay you as a freelancer, to do their work for them. With that, you can take your clan on the road, working wherever you go and traveling between time.

There are a couple of factors which work in your favor, if you choose this sort of a lifestyle. First of all, your cost of living will be much lower than it is today. Assuming that you can sell your home with enough profit to allow you to buy a RV, your main expense is going to be gasoline. Many of your monthly expenses will disappear, allowing you to work less hours and still make enough money for your needs.

Another great advantage of this lifestyle is that it provides you with an excellent opportunity to teach your children survival skills.

There are countless campgrounds across the nation which are located in the woods. State and federal park campgrounds are the best for this. Pick a skill to work on in each campground and hone your family's survival skills as you go.

Then there's what I've already mentioned; the fact that most of the time you'll already be bugged out. As long as you keep track of the news, you'll know what's going on and what to avoid. So you should be able to avoid most problems. If it looks like a hurricane is coming into the Gulf Cost, and you happen to be in that area, all you have to do is move inland, before everyone else does. Pick a campground and settle in to wait out the storm.

The one drawback to this system, is a lack of storage space in the RV. If you try and downsize from a home to an RV, you'll have to get rid of a lot of what you're used to using. That means that you won't have a lot of room for a stockpile of emergency supplies. However, if you plan properly, you can still bring several months along with you.

They can be in the under-coach storage, in roof pods or under beds. Or, you could bring along a cargo trailer to carry your stockpile.

Another option is to set up caches of supplies in various storage areas, in areas that you frequent. That way, if things get bad, you'll always have supplies that you can access, as long as you can get to them. With several such locations, you should be in good shape, no matter what comes your way.

Chapter 12:
Considerations for Families

Bugging out is difficult for anyone. The challenges of getting away from home, coupled with living in the wilderness off of what nature provides can challenge the best of us. In the past, this was best undertaken by single men, at least until the country was opened up by them. But bugging out with a family takes what is normally difficult and adds whole new dimensions of problems.

Even the Lord recognized this and made mention of it when he was talking about bugging out. I quoted His statement from Luke on that earlier, but he also talks about it in Matthew. There he says:

> *And woe unto them that are with child, and to them that give suck in those days!* [20] *But pray ye that your flight be not in the winter, neither on the sabbath day: Matthew 24:19-20*

Anyone who is a parent knows that raising children is a challenge. But could you imagine trying to raise children in conditions that require you to bug out? Not only would you have to do all the normal things you would do at home, but you'd have to provide for them in less than ideal circumstances, while protecting them from everything that nature can throw at them.

Yet you can't abandon your children. God has entrusted them to you for a purpose, so you have to plan for them and plan how you are going to take care of them in those circumstances. This is critical, because failure to plan is usually followed by failure.

To start with, you need to prepare your children for the eventuality of bugging out. That means a little bit of physical conditioning, so that they can walk a long distance, as well as preparing them mentally for the idea of leaving home and living out in the woods. You can make this much easier for them, by simply taking the time to do just that; go spend time in the woods, training them.

Camping is a great opportunity to teach the necessary skills for wilderness survival, without having the risks associated with having to survive. You can teach your children how to make a shelter, how to start a fire, how to purify water, how to fish, how to build a snare and a host of other skills, all under the guise of going out to the woods and going camping for the weekend. Actually, you'll need several weekends, but the more the better.

Make sure you include some good hikes as part of those camping weekends. Let them carry their own pack, albeit a small one. That way, they can get used to the physical strain of it, as well as the idea of walking for several hours. The more you do, the more they will be strengthened and prepared.

Don't forget to teach your children how to shoot, either. Children can actually start shooting rather young, if they are responsible enough to understand gun safety. Start them light, with a .22 caliber rifle and work up from there.

No matter what happens, they will undoubtedly need the ability to use a firearm, both for hunting and self-defense, if things get bad enough that you have to bug out.

Keep in mind that children will slow you down in your travels. How much they slow you down will depend a lot on their age and physical condition. Babies are the worst, as you have to carry them or take them along in a stroller. As your children grow, they will gradually become better conditioned and better prepared to hold up their own end of the stick, becoming useful members of your survival team. As teens, you should be able to teach them to the point where they can survive on their own.

When planning your escape route, do so with the limitations of your children in mind. It is quite possible that you will only be able to make three or four miles a day, not the 10 to 20 you could make alone. But if that's the situation, you have to live with it.

You also need to plan on teaching and training your children, once you are out in the wild. Their education is important to them, especially to their future. Even if the world as we know it comes to an end, they will need skills to live and make a living.

Teaching the basics of reading, writing and arithmetic doesn't require a whole lot. Hopefully you remember those lessons yourself, well enough to teach them to your children. Bring a Bible with you and teach them about the Lord. Many a child in our country's history learned to read by reading the stories of the Bible. This would be an excellent time to return to that tradition. But also teach them the skills they need to help rebuild society. What do you know, that they should? Teach them as much as you can, in the time you can; because the day will come when you won't be there to do it for them.

A strong family can survive together. There's a reason why God created the family unit, and that reason is for the children. As parents, we are charged with the responsibility of preparing the next generation, with the idea that they will go farther than we have and accomplish more than we do. Only you can do that; nobody else can do that for you.

Chapter 13: Conclusion

The conclusion of this book is actually the beginning of your journey. Now is the time to take massive action and get things done again not out of the spirit of fear, but out of the spirit of love using your sound mind that God has given you. We will all go through different spurts and times in which we feel anxious, worried or fearful and these are the times that try men's souls - yet as you cling ever closer to Christ and His word you will have the peace of God that surpasses all understanding for God cannot lie when he promises in His Word is an unstoppable truth.

We have covered a lot of subjects throughout this book yet to be quite honest we've only scratched the surface.

I hope that you use this book as it's intended, for the purpose of this book is for you and your family to get prepared as best as possible from a Christian perspective, to give you the operational framework that is necessary instead of going through all of the craziness to put the pieces of the puzzle together – I hope in some small way this helps put the pieces of the puzzle together that much quicker for you and that you truly gain the necessary understanding that God wants for you. For God does not desire for His people to be ignorant – what does the word of God say, my people perish for lack of knowledge. God doesn't want His people to perish but to have an intimate personal relationship with Him through understanding the Word of God.

I hope you will also pass on this book to potentially a nonbeliever in Jesus Christ who may be receptive to information regarding prepping and preparedness – again our greatest prep, our greatest asset if you would in our life should be Jesus Christ and even now I still implore you to come to Jesus right now while you yet still can, while there is still hope for change in Christ Jesus, while you yet still have breath in your lungs to speak the words that can bring everlasting healing, hope, peace, and everlasting life – do it now my friend. For God said in an acceptable time I've heard your cry and helped you - behold now is the time for salvation, behold now is the time.

This is the American Christian Defense Alliance, Inc. attempt to help warn and prepare you before it's too late – We have done our part, Now what will you do?

Special Gift

God has a Gift for You!   The Plan of Salvation:

There is no formal prayer of salvation as many churches would have you believe, God's Word is very clear - there is only one way to get to the Father in heaven and that is through Jesus Christ (John 14:6). Jesus says that you must be born again to enter into heaven (John 3:3-5).

Salvation is simply the first step in building an open and honest relationship with God. We all have sinned and fallen short, but there is Hope in Jesus Christ - Just cry out to God in sincerity and honesty asking for forgiveness and for Him to Save you, Sanctify you, and fill you with His Holy Spirit - Ask for His will to be done in your life on earth as it is in Heaven and That's it, now just keep it real with God.

A Warning:

The Christian walk is not an easy life on the surface. The Word of God says that we will be hated in all the world for Christ namesake (Matt. 24:9). The Bible says that in the last days are enemy prevail against us physically until Christ returns to save us (Dan 7:21, 22). Furthermore, we must endure hardship as a good soldier of Jesus Christ (2 Tim 2:3) and yet we are never alone in this, God promises us that He will never leave us nor forsake us if we believe in him (Matt.28:20).

In everything we go through we have the peace and joy of God which surpasses all understanding (Philp. 4:6-8) The Bible declares, "For I consider the sufferings of this present time are not worthy to be compared with the glory which shall be revealed in us". (Rom 8:18). However, in all these things we are more than conquerors through Jesus Christ (Rom. 8:37)

Stay In Contact

Our Contact Information

Stay in Contact with the American Christian Defense Alliance, Inc. though Our Website At: www.ACDAInc.Org

Join Our Mailing List

We also Greatly Appreciate You Signing Up For Our Mailing List and Providing a Good Rating and Review for this Book. Your Reviews help other people like yourself find this book and benefit from its contents.

If You or Your Family have been Blessed by this book please let us know by dropping us a line through our website at http://acdainc.org

Thanks Again for Reading

God Bless!

Find All Our Books

Our Books:

Get the Entire 7 Book Series of Bible Studies for Belts

Martial Arts Ministry: How To Start A Martial Arts Ministry

Prayer: Your No. 1 Prayer Book To Learn To Be A Strong Christian Prayer Warrior That Prays With Powerful Prayers In The War Room To Overcome And Defeat The Enemy

Real Men Don't Make Promises: Understanding Oaths, Pacts, Covenants & Promises From A Biblical Perspective

A Vague Notion: How To Overcome Limiting Beliefs of Fear and Anxiety Through the Word of God

Biblical Bug Out: Don't Bug In - Follow The Calling

Christian Prepping 101: How To Start Prepping

Prepping: A Christian Perspective

Prepping: Survival Basics

Bug Out: Prepper Preparations for Survival, SHTF, Natural Disasters, Off Grid Living, Civil Unrest, and Martial Law to Help You Survive the End Times

Overcoming 50 Shades of Grey And All The Colors Of The LGBT Rainbow: How To Conquer Your Lust and Walk In The Spirit Of God

Salvation for Your Unsaved Mom: 10 Things to Tell Your Mom Before She Dies

Parenting: How To Be A Great Parent And Raise Awesome Kids

How To Finance Your Full-Time RV Dream

Prayer
Your No. 1 Prayer Book To Learn To Be A Strong Christian Prayer Warrior That Prays With Powerful Prayers In The War Room To Overcome And Defeat The Enemy

By: Patrick Baldwin

COPYRIGHT © 2017
AMERICAN CHRISTIAN DEFENSE ALLIANCE, INC.
Baltimore, Maryland
ACDAINC.ORG

ALL RIGHTS RESERVED. NO PART OF THIS PUBLICATION MAY BE REPRODUCED IN ANY FORM OR BY ANY MEANS, INCLUDING SCANNING, PHOTOCOPYING, OR OTHERWISE WITHOUT PRIOR WRITTEN PERMISSION OF THE COPYRIGHT HOLDER.

Disclaimer

This book is a guide to help you strengthen your prayer life – it is not intended to guarantee that God will answer your prayers. Often times when God doesn't answer our prayers it is in fact an answer to prayers. Yet not too many of us realize this reality, we feel if God doesn't answer our prayers something's wrong and we often question – why? The truth of the matter is we may never know the why here on this side of heaven, but rest in the promises of God for He is faithful and just to take you from glory to glory and that He will direct your steps along the way as you continue to pray. God does not forsake His children but at times chastises them much like a tree in need of pruning. It doesn't always feel good and it's not always pleasant but most assuredly we know we can trust in God no matter what.

Unfortunately in today's society I have to put this disclaimer in this book so everyone has a clear understanding that I make no promise, guarantee, or assurance whether directly or indirectly that God will answer any of your prayers – that is completely and totally at the sole discretion of Almighty God, the Alpha and Omega, the great I am.

Furthermore it should be completely understood as previously mentioned that often times when we pray and we don't see God answering our prayers God is in fact answering our prayers for He knows the things that you have need of even before you ask. This is a critical concept to understand for we may pray an error or contrary to God's will for life but thanks be to God who leads us and guides us despite our ignorance.

Special Request

Thank you for purchasing our book and supporting our Ministry. We actually have two requests – To Pray for Our Ministry and to Read this Book All the Way through. No Ministry can survive without Prayer and Support so we ask you to keep our Ministry in Your Daily Prayers and Pray as the Lord leads.

We encourage you to Read the Book you purchased all the way through. Many Books NEVER Get Read, and the ones that do only get read the first few pages.

One of our Special Request is that if you are serious about learning the material in this book that you take time to actually read this book in its entirety – all the way through.

We all lead such busy lives nowadays and can get side tracked so easily please take a moment to consider my words and read to the end of the book and keep us in Your Prayers.

Thank You once again for purchase. We deeply appreciate Your Prayers and Support and know that God will Bless You as You continue to Bless this Ministry.

Dedication

This Book is dedicated to My Mom

~May You Rest in Peace (May 25, 1950 – November 10, 2016)~

This Book is Also Dedicated to Every Prayer Warrior Out there who Continues to Stand in the Gap and Pray for those Around them – God Bless You.

Forward

Prayer, along with the written Word (the Bible) is the most valuable tool we have when it comes to formulating a personal relationship with The Lord. The reason these two things are so essential can be summed up in one word—communication. It not only allows us to hear God, but communication is a two-way street. And prayer is the 'street' that allows us to communicate back to God.

Prayer is also the most misused, misunderstood, and un-used resource we have available to us. God created us in His image. His image! Do you understand what that means? It means we are as like God as any aspect of creation can be. It means we are special. It means God very much desires to have a relationship with us—one that is deeply personal. It means He will listen and answer our prayers when we pray because of His desire to be close to us.

You don't ignore your spouse, your children, your friends, or your boss when they talk to you, do you? Of course not! You also expect them to listen to you when you have something to say. So why do you think it should be any different with God? The answer to that question is this: It shouldn't be. Your willingness to talk to God and to have Him talk to you should be even greater than it is with the other relationships you have in your life.

The purpose of this book is to help you achieve that goal. By looking at what prayer is, how to pray, what to pray for, and when to pray, you will hopefully become more equipped and fully aware of what it means to pray to God and overcome and defeat the spiritual enemy.

Chapter 1: What is Prayer?

Prayer is conversation between you and God. It is both speaking and listening. You speak. God listens. God speaks. You listen.

You speak

Prayer is the time you spend talking to God about the cares and concerns of your heart. It is the time you tell Him the desires of your heart. It is time spent praising God for being His amazing, holy, and wonderful self. It is time spent confessing your sins and asking God's forgiveness. It is time spent talking to God on behalf of family, friends, your church, our government, our military, missionaries, and whoever or whatever else concerns you.

God listens

God listens to each and every word we say. He even listens to our thoughts. Philippians 4:6 says, *Be careful for nothing; but in every thing by prayer and supplication with thanksgiving let your requests be made known unto God.* Did you get that? We can (and should) go to God about everything.

God listened to Elijah when he questioned God's decision to allow the widow's son to die. Once more, God gave Elijah what he asked for: *And he cried unto the Lord, and said, O Lord my God, hast thou also brought evil upon the widow with whom I sojourn, by slaying her son? And he stretched himself upon the child three times, and cried unto the Lord, and said, O Lord my God, I pray thee, let this child's soul come into him again. And the Lord heard the voice of Elijah; and the soul of the child came into him again, and he revived. (1st Kings 17:20-22)*

God listened to Mordecai when he prayed that God would intervene and save the Jewish race from annihilation at the hand of Haman (Esther4:1).

God listened to David when he asked God to forgive him for his sins of adultery and conspiracy for murder. David's prayer asking forgiveness is one of the most beautiful of all the psalms…

Have mercy upon me, O God, according to thy lovingkindness: according unto the multitude of thy tender mercies blot out my transgressions. Wash me throughly from mine iniquity, and cleanse me from my sin. For I acknowledge my transgressions: and my sin is ever before me. Against thee, thee only, have I sinned, and done this evil in thy sight: that thou mightest be justified when thou speakest, and be clear when thou judgest…

Purge me with hyssop, and I shall be clean: wash me, and I shall be whiter than snow. Make me to hear joy and gladness; that the bones which thou hast broken may rejoice. Hide thy face from my sins, and blot out all mine iniquities. Create in me a clean heart, O God; and renew a right spirit within me. Cast me not away from thy presence; and take not thy holy spirit from me. Restore unto me the joy of thy salvation; and uphold me with thy free spirit. (Psalm 51:1-4 and 7-12)

God listened to Jesus when He asked God to forgive those who were responsible for His death when He said, *"Then said Jesus, Father, forgive them; for they know not what they do." (Luke 23:34)*

God speaks

When we pray, we're not the only ones doing the talking. God does plenty of talking when we pray. No, we don't audibly hear God's voice like Abraham, Moses, Jonah, and numerous others did normally. But we hear God in that little voice that speaks to our heart and to our mind; telling us to do what we know is right and good. God's voice is the voice that warns us against sin and encourages us to go in the direction He created us to go.

Abraham's servant prayed to God; asking Him to provide the right woman for him to take home for Isaac to marry…

And he said O Lord God of my master Abraham, I pray thee, send me good speed this day, and shew kindness unto my master Abraham. Behold, I stand here by the well of water; and the daughters of the men of the city come out to draw water: And let it come to pass, that the damsel to whom I shall say,

Let down thy pitcher, I pray thee, that I may drink; and she shall say, Drink, and I will give thy camels drink also: let the same be she that thou hast appointed for thy servant Isaac; and thereby shall I know that thou hast shewed kindness unto my master. (Genesis 24:12-14)

God spoke to this man by giving him exactly what he asked for—a clear and definite answer as to the girl he was to take home to Isaac.

God audibly spoke to Moses countless times. One that especially stands out in my mind was the time God was so angry at the Israelites for building the golden calf and worshipping it that He told Moses He was going to kill them all and start over—creating a nation of people from Moses rather than Abraham. Let's look at this incident and then talk about it some more…

And the Lord said unto Moses, Go, get thee down; for thy people, which thou broughtest out of the land of Egypt, have corrupted themselves: They have turned aside quickly out of the way which I commanded them: they have made them a molten calf, and have worshipped it, and have sacrificed thereunto, and said, These be thy gods, O Israel, which have brought thee up out of the land of Egypt. And the Lord said unto Moses, I have seen this people, and, behold, it is a stiffnecked people: Now therefore let me alone, that my wrath may wax hot against them, and that I may consume them: and I will make of thee a great nation. And Moses besought the Lord his God, and said, Lord, why doth thy wrath wax hot against thy people, which thou hast brought forth out of the land of Egypt with great power, and with a mighty hand? Wherefore should the Egyptians speak, and say, For mischief did he bring them out, to slay them in the mountains, and to consume them from the face of the earth?

Turn from thy fierce wrath, and repent of this evil against thy people. Remember Abraham, Isaac, and Israel, thy servants, to whom thou swarest by thine own self, and saidst unto them, I will multiply your seed as the stars of heaven, and all this land that I have spoken of will I give unto your seed, and they shall inherit it for ever. And the Lord repented of the evil which he thought to do unto his people. (Exodus 2:7-14)

Some might say this wasn't actually a prayer, but considering the fact that prayer is conversation between us and God, I'd say it most definitely was. Keeping that in mind, let's take a more in-depth look at what God was *saying* to Moses in this brief encounter:

- God is instructing Moses; telling him to go down to the people.
- God is voicing his anger and hurt because Israel was so quick to turn their backs on God.

- It would have been or at least tempting (to some degree) for Moses to say, "Go ahead! Wipe them out and make me the new root of your people." But Moses didn't do that. Moses once again proved himself to be the humble servant of God he was. He reminded God of the promise He made to Abraham and telling God that he was trusting in Him to keep that promise.
- God voiced his pleasure with Moses in being so faithful and humble. He then did just what He had promised Abraham and allowed the Israelites to live.

God spoke to Paul when He didn't give Paul what he asked for—to take away whatever chronic ailment (thorn in the flesh) Paul was dealing with.

He wanted Paul to understand that he could be just as effective (if not more so) in the ministry with the ailment as he could without it. God wanted Paul to remember that the work he was doing was *through* him (Paul) *by* God.

FYI: God wants us to know the same.

You listen

The listening part of prayer on our part can be summed up in one word. Obedience.

Jonah didn't listen to God and paid a pretty steep price for his disobedience (Jonah 1). In spite of Jonah's disobedience God still listened to Jonah and gave him another chance.

Ezekiel obeyed God; leading him to have to do some incredibly awkward, humiliating, and 'interesting' things.

Jesus listened to God throughout His life and ministry here on earth, but never so obviously as He did the night He was arrested. Prior to His arrest, Jesus prayed; asking if there was any other way to bring about salvation for you and me. God said no, and Jesus' reply was "Your will be done".

The act of prayer is an act of communication, but it is also what we call a spiritual discipline. The term itself is not found in the Bible, but is one the Church uses to define those things necessary to become more mature and solid in your relationship with God. They are things we need to make part of our character and normal daily lives. You can see by the definition that prayer most certainly falls into that category.

Chapter 2: How to Pray

Jesus out and out told us how we should pray in the Sermon on the Mount (Matthew 5-7). We refer to this instruction in how to pray as the Lord's Prayer. His instruction is primarily what to pray *for* or *about* rather than actually how to pray, so we're going to save that passage of scripture for another chapter. Instead, we're going to look at how to pray as in what our attitude and approach to prayer should be.

Approaching God in Faith

Let's look at a few verses in the Bible on the subject of approaching God in prayer in faith. In doing so we will discover that faith is the key to hearing and receiving God's answers to our prayers.

Therefore I say unto you, What things soever ye desire, when ye pray, believe that ye receive them, and ye shall have them. ~Mark 11:24

This one (and similar verses) are most likely the most misunderstood verse in the Bible. If not, it definitely rates in the top three. Why? Because it is taken out of context, that's why. If you read the verses just prior to this, you will find that Jesus is speaking to the disciples about faith. He tells them that if they have a strong enough faith they can do anything in His name. He then tells them that whatever they ask for they can have, as well. But this is what is called an implied statement. Jesus is implying (not specifically mentioning because the suggestion or understanding is already there) that they wouldn't ask for anything outside the perimeters of one living a faithful, obedient life.

In other words, you wouldn't ask for things that would draw your heart, soul, and mind away from the Father or the Son. You would ask for things (material and otherwise) that would be of physical, emotional, and spiritual benefit to you and to others.

And this is the confidence that we have in him, that, if we ask any thing according to his will, he heareth us: and if we know that he hear us, whatsoever we ask, we know that we have the petitions that we desired of him. `1st John 5:14-15

If ye abide in me, and my words abide in you, ye shall ask what ye will, and it shall be done unto you. ~John 15:7

And all things, whatsoever ye shall ask in prayer, believing, ye shall receive. ~Matthew 21:22

Both of these verses are also on the end of Jesus' comments about the need for faith and being one with Him—heart, soul, and mind.

But let him ask in faith, nothing wavering. For he that wavereth is like a wave of the sea driven with the wind and tossed. For let not that man think that he shall receive any thing of the Lord. A double minded man is unstable in all his ways. ~James 1:6-8

Praying without having faith is like stopping at all the green lights because you don't have faith they will stay green long enough for you to make it through the intersection.

But without faith it is impossible to please him: for he that cometh to God must believe that he is, and that he is a rewarder of them that diligently seek him. ~Hebrews 11:6

This is one of the most beautiful yet telling verses in the Bible. God promises to reward anyone who diligently seeks Him, but reminds us that this is not possible unless we have a faith that is rock-solid. He knows there will be times when we question whether

He is listening because we aren't getting the results we want when we want them. The faith He is talking about here is the faith that never loses sight of the fact that God is real, holy, almighty – and ultimately in control.

Pray Persistently

Pray without ceasing. ~1st Thessalonians 5:17

Call unto me, and I will answer thee, and show thee great and mighty things, which thou knowest not. ~Jeremiah 33:3

Keep asking. Keep talking. Keep listening. God will answer by giving you the promptings of the Holy Spirit, through the works and encouragement of others, and through the events in your life that too many people chalk up to coincidence, happenstance, and fate.

And he spake a parable unto them to this end, that men ought always to pray, and not to faint; Saying, There was in a city a judge, which feared not God, neither regarded man: And there was a widow in that city; and she came unto him, saying, Avenge me of mine adversary. And he would not for a while: but afterward he said within himself, Though I fear not God, nor regard man; yet because this widow troubleth me, I will avenge her, lest by her continual coming she weary me. And the Lord said, Hear what the unjust judge saith. And shall not God avenge his own elect, which cry day and night unto him, though he bear long with them? I tell you that he will avenge them speedily. Nevertheless when the Son of man cometh, shall he find faith on the earth? ~Luke 18:1-18

Jesus' parable is a reminder that God often wants or needs to know how serious or determined we are for what we pray for. Are we genuinely ready for whatever? Are we resolved to handle His answer?

Pray in Agreement with God

Delight thyself also in the Lord: and he shall give thee the desires of thine heart. ~Psalm 37:4

When we are living obediently and faithfully to God, He will give us the desires of our heart because the first desire of our heart will be to do God's will and those that follow will be in line with what God created us to do and be.

Confess your faults one to another, and pray one for another, that ye may be healed. The effectual fervent prayer of a righteous man availeth much. ~James 5:16

For if ye forgive men their trespasses, your heavenly Father will also forgive you: But if ye forgive not men their trespasses, neither will your Father forgive your trespasses. ~Matthew 6:14-15

God cannot and will not answer the prayers of those who refuse to confess their sins to Him or those who refuse to forgive those who have sinned against them.

If my people, which are called by my name, shall humble themselves, and pray, and seek my face, and turn from their wicked ways; then will I hear from heaven, and will forgive their sin, and will heal their land. ~2nd Chronicles 7:14

We must be willing to humble ourselves to the authority and sovereignty of God. We must acknowledge God as the giver of all *because it is all His to give*.

Pray Expecting Answers

My voice shalt thou hear in the morning, O Lord; in the morning will I direct my prayer unto thee, and will look up. ~Psalm 5:3

David looked up because he knew God was going to answer him. He just knew. I love that because it just shows how sure David was of his God. We should be just as sure today.

Be careful for nothing; but in every thing by prayer and supplication with thanksgiving let your requests be made known unto God. And the peace of God, which passeth all understanding, shall keep your hearts and minds through Christ Jesus. ~Philippians 4:6-7

He shall call upon me, and I will answer him: I will be with him in trouble; I will deliver him, and honour him. ~Psalm 91:15

The promise of God should be enough to let us know that our prayers will be answered.

It is important to remember, though, that answered prayer isn't always answered the way we want or think it should be.

No parent always tells their child yes, so why should God be any different? He is the God of the 'big picture'. He knows what is going to be and what is best for us in the days, weeks, and years ahead.

But they that wait upon the Lord shall renew their strength; they shall mount up with wings as eagles; they shall run, and not be weary; and they shall walk, and not faint. ~Isaiah 40:31

God's timing is always the perfect timing. We need to remember this—to not get tired of waiting and to not refuse the strength and comfort He offers while we wait. We must also be mindful of not refusing to see God's answer to our prayer if it differs from what we think it should be.

If not, hearken unto me: hold thy peace, and I shall teach thee wisdom. ~Job 33:33

This verse from Job reminds us that in order for God to answer our prayers we have to be quiet long enough to hear Him. Job wanted answers but was too busy telling God he wanted them to hear God speaking. But God got Job's attention—just like He will get ours.

In faith, with persistence and expectation and a heart that longs to be right with God—this is the 'recipe' for how to pray.

Chapter 3: Why Pray

We know what Prayer is and How to Pray . . . But Why Pray? Answering the Why is to understand the motivation behind your actions let me start out by asking this, why do you talk to your best friend, your spouse, your employer, or other people around you? Now sometimes you may not want to talk to your spouse, your employer or even your best friend because of whatever issues that are between you or maybe because you know you're in trouble with your employer.

The fact remains, however, despite whatever the circumstances are in our daily life between these individuals we have to communicate and interact with them just about every day. Why should it be any different with your relationship with God – the one that created you and gave you life?

The short answer is it should not be any different, well let me back up, it should be different if you truly know who God is. So that's the question, who is God to you? When you answer this question you're going to be one step closer to answering a very personal question, why pray? Now sure there are basic reasons why we should all pray but it really boils down to your relationship with God and who God is to you. The more that you read His Word, the more that you spend time with God in prayer, the more that you draw close to Him the more the God will mean to you.

Recently Valentine's Day had just passed, now I'm not a fan of this particular holiday if that's what you want to call it because I feel that you should be showing your love each and every day to the person that you're with. Nevertheless it brings me to a point to help you better understand something here.

For those that are married do you remember falling in love with your spouse? Do you remember what it was like to have that all-consuming desire and love for them? Do you remember how you couldn't wait until you were able to see them again or talk with them again? We need to have a love relationship with Jesus Christ in a similar fashion. Now I am not talking about a romantic love but a passionate love nonetheless that seeks to have a servant's heart and a sincere desire to do God's will.

Interesting enough if we look at couples that have been married for a long period of time often times you will find the spark has died, they may barely see each other because of work, and hardly ever speak except for talking about the necessities of life such as bills and the kids. This is a great example of how most of our prayer lives are with God.

We have to get back that spark – do you remember when you first came to the Lord how passionate and on fire you were to serve Him and to pray and communicate with him?

Brothers and sisters it's time for a revival within each of us and then collectively as we organically come together in the spirit – let's start a resurrection and a revival once again, and let it start right now within each of us. And then you will understand why you need to pray.

Continuing on with the relationship theme, how many marriages end in divorce because of adultery, abuse or neglect? How many of us have a prayer life that is in similar disarray?

If you're not praying to God but you're sitting in front of the television for hours each day or listening to music is this not adultery if you do not make equal time for God? Are you abusing your relationship with God by only coming to Him in prayer when you need or want something? Are you neglecting your relationship with Almighty God potentially because of sin that is crêpe in and now hold you captive?

Let me explain how the pattern works brothers and sisters first it starts with neglect then it leads to abuse and ultimately adultery or idolatry as the Bible describes it. It's a vicious cycle but one that can be broken with the blood of the lamb, one that can be broken through committing yourself to learning and getting close to God both in His Word and in Prayer.

Why Pray? Well here's some basic answers:

- Because You Love God
- To Keep Your Relationship with God Strong
- Because You love your family, friends, country etc
- Because you want to see God's will done on Earth as it is in heaven
- To Fight Back Against your Spiritual Enemy
- To Walk in the Authority God has Given You

Remember, prayer is a tangible real thing that should not be discarded or put to the side until you have an emergency or crisis. Is that the kind of relationship you want someone to have with you? Learn to have a good relationship with God by talking with Him daily in prayer.

So many of us continue to struggle and have such a poor prayer life because we don't recognize prayer for what it truly is and just how powerful it is. It should not be your last resort – it should be your immediate response to situations, circumstances, and dealing with our spiritual enemy's attacks.

You must learn to see these attacks for what they are and address them accordingly in prayer – taking authority over the enemy in the name of Jesus. How many of us understand and recognize that every single day of our lives we are in a spiritual war and that prayer is essential for living a victorious life in Christ? Now is the time to Pray!

Chapter 4:

Making Time to Pray

Making time to pray is one of the biggest complaints and hurdles Christians say they are faced with. I get it—life is hectic. We have all sorts of people and things vying for our time and attention. It only seems practical or reasonable to put the things that are staring us in the face first. But oh, what a mistake that is!

To help put it into perspective, let me ask you the following questions:

- Would you consider eating dinner and going to bed instead of picking your child up from sports practice or piano lessons because you are at home and able to *see* dinner cooking on the stove and your bedroom, but cannot see your child while they are at practice/lessons?

- Would you consider not paying your insurance premiums in order to buy new furniture because you can see the furniture but not the benefits of having the insurance?
- Would you not call your parents or grandparents to talk with them or check on their well-being if seeing them on a regular basis was not possible? You know, the 'out of sight, out of mind' philosophy?

I am hoping and praying you answered each of these questions with an emphatic NO. Why, then, do you relegate God and prayer to a status of 'bottom of the totem pole' (last place)?

Whether or not you make time to pray shouldn't be the question. The question should be what you have time for *after* you pray. You might have to give up a television show, a few less minutes in the book you are reading, one less round of golf, or take one less class at the gym, but prayer should take precedence over the activities in your life.

How to make time to pray

If your response to the last statement is something resembling denial that you are too busy or that you cannot possibly give up *that,* you seriously need to re-think your priorities. That being said, I don't want you to feel that what you do with your day is of no importance or significance. That is why I want to offer you the following suggestions on how to make time to pray:

- Set aside a special time for prayer each day. A time of completely being focused on conversing with God is essential in your relationship with Him. Think about it: you wouldn't appreciate it if your spouse or your children never took the time to focus on talking to you. You would feel slighted and unimportant. You would feel you were in the way and an inconvenient duty rather than a treasured and cherished loved one.

This is exactly how God feels when we fit Him in when we have a minute here and there or if we are in over our heads and need His divine intervention. By taking the time to be solely focused on prayer each day, you will know God so much more intimately; making it possible for you to avoid many of the issues people use to distance themselves from seeking God's face each day.

- Pray before all Meals and as a Family
- Pray before you drive anywhere and Pray as you are driving: hands on the wheel, eyes on the road, pray for safety, pray for those you meet on the road, pray for the ability to be a witness of God's goodness in all you do and say throughout your day.

- Pray while fixing your kids' breakfast or lunch. Pray for their safety, that they will make right choices, and that they will seek to have a personal relationship with God each and every day of their lives.
- Pray while taking a walk. Pray for your community, your church, our government and military, and for those you know who have specific needs.
- Pray when you first open your eyes each morning. Thank God for the rest you enjoyed, for His amazing grace, for the fact that He is God, and for the precious gift of salvation.
- Pray when you lay your head on the pillow at night. When you make conversation and thoughts of God among the last ones you have each night, you can go to sleep with the peace that passes all understanding.

> FYI: Often time's people say they feel guilty falling asleep at night in the middle of their prayers. But I will share with you something I read a while back on that very subject: nothing could be sweeter than drifting off to sleep while talking with your creator. What better company could you possibly have?

Again, I know it isn't always easy to push the hustle and bustle of life out of the way, but for anyone who claims Jesus as Savior, it is something you simply must do in order to make your words more than just lip service. Making prayer a priority is also worth it - Always worth it.

To give you a bit of encouragement and inspiration take a few minutes to read through the following Bible verses. I also encourage and challenge you to commit at least two or three of them to memory so that they can serve as your reminders each and every day.

Pray without ceasing. ~1ˢᵗ Thessalonians 5:17

Any time is a good time to pray. Prayer can be a few words spoken out loud or mentally spoken. Prayer can be a cry for help, a shout of praise, a desperate plea, or a heart to heart conversation that lasts as long as it needs to last.

Likewise the Spirit also helpeth our infirmities: for we know not what we should pray for as we ought: but the Spirit itself maketh intercession for us with groanings which cannot be uttered. ~Romans 8:26

I know someone whose prayer is simply this: "LORD, I know You know what is best and that all things work out for Your good, so please just give me the faith, courage, and strength to hold on for the ride."

But thou, when thou prayest, enter into thy closet, and when thou hast shut thy door, pray to thy Father which is in secret; and thy Father which seeth in secret shall reward thee openly. ~Matthew 6:6

This is the time we spend in focused, personal prayer.

What is it then? I will pray with the spirit, and I will pray with the understanding also: I will sing with the spirit, and I will sing with the understanding also. ~1st Corinthians 14:15

Prayers can also be songs, short and simple words of praise, and thank-yous for God's protection, comfort, and active presence in situations.

Praying always with all prayer and supplication in the Spirit, and watching thereunto with all perseverance and supplication for all saints ~Ephesians 6:18

As for me, I will call upon God; and the Lord shall save me. Evening, and morning, and at noon, will I pray, and cry aloud: and he shall hear my voice. ~Psalm 55:16-17

Again…there's never a bad time to pray.

Chapter 5:

Praying the Scriptures

What does it mean to 'pray the scriptures'? The best way to explain it is to pray God's will to be done. It sounds simple because it is. It is also something I can show you better than I can tell you.

Praying the scriptures

Praying for a spouse: *And the Lord God said, It is not good that the man should be alone; I will make him an help meet for him.* ~*Genesis 2:18*

Praying to know God's will for your life: *For I know the thoughts that I think toward you, saith the Lord, thoughts of peace, and not of evil, to give you an expected end.* ~*Jeremiah 29:11*

Praying to be more God-centered and a kingdom worker: *But seek ye first the kingdom of God, and his righteousness; and all these things shall be added unto you. ~Matthew 6:33*

Prayer of thanks for your wife: *Whoso findeth a wife findeth a good thing, and obtaineth favour of the LORD. ~Proverbs 18:22*

Pray for increased faith to see God's answers to your prayers: *And blessed is she that believed: for there shall be a performance of those things which were told her from the Lord. ~Luke 1:45*

Pray for Godly parenting skills: *And blessed is she that believed: for there shall be a performance of those things which were told her from the Lord. ~Ephesians 6:4*

Pray for a Godly marriage: *Wives, submit yourselves unto your own husbands, as unto the Lord. Husbands, love your wives, even as Christ also loved the church, and gave himself for it; ~Ephesians 5:22 and 25*

Prayers of thanks for God's gift of salvation: *But God commendeth his love toward us, in that, while we were yet sinners, Christ died for us. ~Romans 5:8*

Pray for the ability to treat those who hurt and persecute you: *But I say unto you, Love your enemies, bless them that curse you, do good to them that hate you, and pray for them which despitefully use you, and persecute you. ~Matthew 5:44*

Prayer of thanks for your friends and loved ones: *I thank my God always on your behalf, for the grace of God which is given you by Jesus Christ ~1st Corinthians 1:4*

Pray for the Church to grow: *Pray ye therefore the Lord of the harvest, that he will send forth labourers into his harvest. ~Matthew 9:38*

Pray to know the mind of Christ for your life: *Ye ask, and receive not, because ye ask amiss, that ye may consume it upon your lusts. ~James 4:3*

Pray for your government and the leaders you work and live under: *I exhort therefore, that, first of all, supplications, prayers, intercessions, and giving of thanks, be made for all men; For kings, and for all that are in authority; that we may lead a quiet and peaceable life in all godliness and honesty. For this is good and acceptable in the sight of God our Saviour; Who will have all men to be saved, and to come unto the knowledge of the truth. ~1st Timothy 2:1-4*

Pray for the lost: *Brethren, my heart's desire and prayer to God for Israel is, that they might be saved. ~Romans 10:1*

Hopefully seeing the scriptures paired with the prayer you can pray helps in understanding what it means to 'pray the scripture'. But just in case it doesn't, here are some examples of what it 'looks like'…

Father, thank You for loving me. Thank You for salvation and your unconditional love. Father, I ask that you give me a heart that seeks Your kingdom and Your righteousness in my life. I pray You will be my first priority in all things because I know when I live my life in this way You will supply all my needs. (Matthew 6:33) In Jesus' name I pray, amen.

Or...

Father, God, You have said that it is not good for man to be alone. That is why I come to you asking for You to send me the someone I can spend my life with. Send me that special someone who I will love and cherish all the days of my life. I pray he/she will be gentle, faithful to You and to me, and that we can work together to raise children who call You LORD. In Jesus' name I pray, amen. (Genesis 2:18)

Why pray the scriptures

Praying the scriptures serves several purposes—all of which are good and serve to help you grow spiritually. Praying the scriptures:

- Keeps you in focus to pray God's will for yourself and for others
- Makes you more knowledgeable of the Word
- Allows you to 'cover all the bases' of prayer (thanksgiving, confession, praise, intercession, petition)
- Gives you a more God-centered attitude about life in general

How to pray the scriptures

Praying the scriptures is often done while reading the Bible or during those times when your prayers are brief conversations with specific concerns and/or observations are being made. For example…

If you were reading the book of Proverbs in your daily Bible reading/study, you might pray, "LORD, let me cry out for wisdom and knowledge as the writer of Proverbs tells me to so that I will understand what it means to fear and respect You." (Proverbs 2:3 & 5)

Or…

When you are moved by the words of the preacher in a worship service, you might pray, "I am not ashamed of the Gospel and I want You to know, God, that I am committed to living and speaking its truth each and every day with bold grace." (Romans 1:16)

Praying the scriptures won't constitute your entire prayer life, but it will definitely enhance its quality and depth.

Chapter 6:

Praying for God's Will to be Done

Similar to praying the Scriptures in the previous chapter, praying for God's will be done is closely related. When you are praying the Scriptures you are praying for specific things that may or may not relate directly to you. God may have specific plans just for you and unfortunately many of us don't know or understand what our calling truly is.

While praying for a wife, wisdom, or the ability to love your enemies are all great things to pray for – what if God's desire for you is not to be married or have children, will you still love Him?

See we don't always get what we want and not everything in Scripture applies directly to us personally -attempting to apply such a philosophy to Scripture would be an error. It's at these crucial times that we literally Pray for God's will to be done on earth as it is in heaven in our lives – in every aspect of our lives. Pray and ask God to open the doors that He would have you walk through and closed the doors tightly that He would not have you walk through.

Remember Praying without believing is like faith without works – one has to accompany the other to be complete and true. Also remember to keep it real with God, do not simply just pay Him lip service – you're literally wasting your breath.

If you're going to pray for God's will to be done on earth as it is in heaven in your life you have to be ready to accept what that means and what comes next. I think many of us lack the necessary courage and faith to walk out God's will for our lives. Praying for the necessary courage and faith to walk it out would no doubt be a great prayer if you find yourself doubting or fearful – pray against those things immediately and take authority over them in Jesus name.

Chapter 7:

Jesus Example of Prayer

Jesus Example of Prayer in John 17:

These words spake Jesus, and lifted up his eyes to heaven, and said, Father, the hour is come; glorify thy Son, that thy Son also may glorify thee: ^{2}As thou hast given him power over all flesh, that he should give eternal life to as many as thou hast given him. ^{3}And this is life eternal, that they might know thee the only true God, and Jesus Christ, whom thou hast sent. ^{4}I have glorified thee on the earth: I have finished the work which thou gavest me to do. ^{5}And now, O Father, glorify thou me with thine own self with the glory which I had with thee before the world was. ^{6}I have manifested thy name unto the men which thou gavest me out of the world: thine they were, and thou gavest them me; and they have kept thy word. ^{7}Now they have known that all things whatsoever thou hast given me are of thee.

⁸ For I have given unto them the words which thou gavest me; and they have received them, and have known surely that I came out from thee, and they have believed that thou didst send me. ⁹ I pray for them: **I pray not for the world**, but for them which thou hast given me; for they are thine. ¹⁰ And all mine are thine, and thine are mine; and I am glorified in them. ¹¹ And now I am no more in the world, but these are in the world, and I come to thee. Holy Father, keep through thine own name those whom thou hast given me, that they may be one, as we are. ¹² While I was with them in the world, I kept them in thy name: those that thou gavest me I have kept, and none of them is lost, but the son of perdition; that the scripture might be fulfilled. ¹³ And now come I to thee; and these things I speak in the world, that they might have my joy fulfilled in themselves. ¹⁴ I have given them thy word; and the world hath hated them, because they are not of the world, even as I am not of the world. ¹⁵ I pray not that thou shouldest take them out of the world, **but that thou shouldest keep them from the evil**.

[16] They are not of the world, even as I am not of the world. [17] **Sanctify them through thy truth: thy word is truth.** [18] As thou hast sent me into the world, even so have I also sent them into the world. [19] And for their sakes I sanctify myself, that they also might be sanctified through the truth. [20] **Neither pray I for these alone, but for them also which shall believe on me through their word;** [21] That they all may be one; as thou, Father, art in me, and I in thee, that they also may be one in us: that the world may believe that thou hast sent me. [22] And the glory which thou gavest me I have given them; that they may be one, even as we are one: [23] I in them, and thou in me, that they may be made perfect in one; and that the world may know that thou hast sent me, and hast loved them, as thou hast loved me. [24] Father, I will that they also, whom thou hast given me, be with me where I am; that they may behold my glory, which thou hast given me: for thou lovedst me before the foundation of the world. [25] O righteous

Father, the world hath not known thee: but I have known thee, and these have known that thou hast sent me. [26] And I have declared unto them thy name, and will declare it: that the love wherewith thou hast loved me may be in them, and I in them.

This may in fact be Jesus's longest prayer that is recorded in the New Testament, let's look at some key things that stand out in this prayer. First and foremost it's important to recognize that in this particular prayer Jesus does not pray for the world but for those that believe in Him – His disciples and those that would believe because of the disciple's words. Jesus also prays that his father would keep them from evil and sanctify them through God's word. It's amazing that over 2000 years ago when Christ prayed these words that He was thinking about you and I who believe in Him because of the apostles words written down in the Holy Bible. What an awesome God we serve.

In this prayer we read how Jesus interacts with the father – does your prayer life look like this? How do you pray for the disciples that you should be making? How do you pray for future generations that will believe because of those disciples' words? Are you even making disciples? Are you going about your father's business – will you hear the words well done good and faithful servant? In this prayer Jesus knows He is about to return back to the father and that His time is short, it's almost like He's reviewing a checklist for things that he needed to do while He was on earth.

We, however, do not know when our time on this earth will be completed therefore it is critical to pray with a sense of urgency as if eternity is just around the corner. The more that you study this specific prayer the more you will have insight into the heart of Jesus Christ.

"The Lord's Prayer"

Jesus' words to His disciples in regards to instructing them (and us) how to pray are what we refer to as the Lord's Prayer. The passage of scripture found in Matthew 6 is often recited and memorized as an actual prayer. Quite honestly, however, this is not what it was intended to be. Jesus' intentions weren't for us to recite His words. His intentions were for us to pattern our prayers according to His outline'.

This might bring up the question of whether or not it is wrong to pray the Lord's Prayer. My answer to that would be no—that it is not *wrong*, but I would add to that by saying it is not really beneficial to do so. I say this because:

- The Lord's Prayer is not *personal* and from the heart—as prayer should be.
- Praying the Lord's Prayer might be considered praying the scripture, but unless you make it specific, you are reciting, not praying.

That being said…the Lord's Prayer is a good way to teach yourself or others how to stay focused on praying for and about the things we need to pray for. So let's take a look at the Lord's Prayer; taking it apart line by line to see what Jesus is wanting us to learn from His model prayer.

After this manner therefore pray ye: Our Father which art in heaven, Hallowed be thy name. Thy kingdom come, Thy will be done in earth, as it is in heaven. Give us this day our daily bread. And forgive us our debts, as we forgive our debtors. And lead us not into temptation, but deliver us from evil: For thine is the kingdom, and the power, and the glory, forever. Amen. ~Matthew 6:9-13

Our Father in heaven, hallowed be thy name: Recognizing God for who He is should always be first in your daily prayer sessions. When you recognize God you are naturally humbled. Doing so also prepares your heart for speaking, listening, and obeying because it affirms your faith and belief in God's holiness.

God isn't picky when it comes to what you say to 'hallow His name'. A simple thank-you for being God will do, but it isn't difficult to come up with a whole lot more than that. You can also praise God for His holiness by recognizing any of the many attributes of His character. For example, some of the character traits the Bible attributes to God include:

- Personally interested—God is personally interested in every little detail of your life. He has the hairs on your head numbered as well as the days of your life. He has a lot invested in you and is constantly watching and waiting for a return on that investment.
- Creator of all—all of creation is God's to do with as He pleases. To praise God for the intricate workings of nature should be as natural as breathing.

- Vine pruner—God prunes and shapes our lives so that we can live out our purpose. Discipline is a part of growing and maturing. To expect otherwise is prideful and honestly, quite delusional. Who are we to think God shouldn't correct us? When done correctly, discipline is an excellent teacher as well as serving to hone our skills and character. FYI: God always 'does discipline' the right way.
- Truth—God's Word is true and unchanging and He is always good for the many promises He has made.
- Savior—God's mercy and unconditional love are the only reason we have salvation from sin that offers the opportunity to spend eternity with Him.
- Eternal—God is forever and nothing is going to change that.
- Forgiving—when we sincerely ask forgiveness God is always ready, willing, and able to forgive. This is the greatest attribute of all.

Thy kingdom come, Thy will be done in earth, as it is in heaven. I am quite certain that most people reciting these words don't truly understand what it is they are saying or asking for. I am also equally certain they don't realize the responsibility they are signing on for when they say these words. I don't say this to be critical or to sound as if I am on a higher level of spirituality. I am simply trying to help each of us come to a more intimate and genuine level of communication with God. So let's take a closer look at this phrase and what it really means…

Thy kingdom come. Jesus is really saying two things here.

1) He is saying we should be praying with anticipation for God to sound the trumpet for the second coming of Christ. That's pretty straightforward and easy to understand. But it is also something many people *say* they look forward to, but…

To ask God to come soon should come from a heart that truly looks forward with assurance and hope for eternity in heaven.

2) Jesus is also talking about the growth of the Kingdom of God here on earth. In many of Jesus' parables He says "..the kingdom of God…" or "…the kingdom of heaven...". In both instances Jesus is referring to you and me here as in the body of saved believers. He is instructing us to pray for the development of the Kingdom of God within us and for the Kingdom to grow and spread across the world so that as many as possible might come to know Jesus as Savior. This is definitely something we should be praying for.

Now for our role in this: in praying for the growth and spreading of the Kingdom of God, we are saying we will do our part to make that happen.

We are basically saying, "Bring on the Great Commission! I'm ready to get down to the business of making Disciples!"

But are you? Am I? Are we really willing to help God's kingdom increase here on earth? If so, what are we actively doing to try to make that happen in our own little corner of the world?

Thy will be done in earth, as it is in heaven. This is simply Jesus' way of emphasizing what He had just said—to remind us that God's kingdom wasn't just some far-off place. Jesus was reminding us that we have a job to do here on earth and that job is to be God's living, breathing, and active representatives of His Kingdom. We are to be about the business of God each and every day of our lives. This sentence in the model prayer is to remind us that we shouldn't be shy or scared to ask God for a daily supply of courage, strength, wisdom, compassion, discernment, and love to be who and what we are supposed to be.

Give us this day our daily bread. We are to ask God for the things we need—bread and everything else.

Sometimes we are so naïve. Or maybe it's pride. Either way we are often blind to the fact that everything we have belongs to God. He gives us the ability to earn a salary from which we buy the things we enjoy and have to have, but it all goes back to the fact that *He gives us the ability.*

Asking God to provide our needs and the desires of our heart humbles us to recognize our inability to make due on our own and the fact that these things are God's to give as He pleases. We are expressing our need for God's care and provision.

And forgive us our debts, as we forgive our debtors. The words 'debt' and 'debtors' in the original Greek means 'that which is due'. Using this direct translation of the word, let's look at what Jesus is saying:

Forgive us for not giving You that which is due in the same way we forgive those who don't give us that which is due us.

I see a bit of Jesus' irony coming out here. He is instructing us to ask God for the same measure of forgiveness we extend to others. Ouch!

By instructing us in this way, Jesus is reminding us of three things:

1) Jesus is reminding us of our need for grace—that none of us is any more deserving of God's favor than the person next to us.
2) Jesus is reminding us that we are all sinners and that in God's eyes no sin is greater than another.
3) Jesus is reminding us of what He had just said about loving our enemies, not holding grudges, and going the extra mile (Matthew 5).

Immediately following the model for prayer, Jesus goes on to say this:

For if ye forgive men their trespasses, your heavenly Father will also forgive you: But if ye forgive not men their trespasses, neither will your Father forgive your trespasses.
~Matthew 6:14-15

The word 'trespasses' in the Greek is translated 'to step over' or 'sin'. I'm not sure why He used the word 'trespass' here and the word 'debtor' in giving us the model prayer, but it is obvious He is tying the two together. He knows that an unforgiving heart cannot be in alignment with doing the will of God. That is why He instructed us to pray this for ourselves each and every day.

And lead us not into temptation, but deliver us from evil... When I read this I think of the old hymn, "I Need Thee Every Hour". Part of it goes like this:

I need Thee every hour; stay close and nearby. Temptations lose their power when You are close by. I need Thee, Oh, I need Thee. Every hour I need Thee. Oh, bless me now my Savior, I come to Thee.

The Bible tells us in no uncertain terms that neither God nor Jesus tempts us—that temptation comes from the devil. He plants it like seeds in our hearts and minds. He puts it before us in cunning disguises, but it is always from him. The devil is also very persuasive in his ability to tempt us. Jesus knows that. He also knows that we need to stay in prayer if we are going to walk in victory against the devil and his minions.

For thine is the kingdom, and the power, and the glory, forever. Amen. The ending of our prayer should be to bring it full-circle; putting the focus back on God. Ending our prayer time by giving God the glory and recognition he deserves is only fitting. Ending our prayers this way also serves as just one more reminder of the fact that we are reliant on and hopeful in God.

There are a number of things people do to assist them in establishing a consistent prayer life. We're going to look at several of them in the next chapter, but I want to close this section of the book by saying that when it comes to the 'mechanics' of prayer, Jesus' model prayer is much more than an idea or suggestion. It is an instruction…command, even…from Jesus the Savior and only Son of God.

Chapter 8:

Learning to be a Prayer Warrior

A prayer warrior—sounds a little intimidating, doesn't it? Don't worry, though. It's not. A prayer warrior is merely a term used to describe someone who is vigilant and ceaseless in their prayers. A prayer warrior is someone who knows and counts on the power of prayer to bring about change and blessing in their life and the lives of others. A Prayer Warrior is someone who understands there is a Spiritual War going on all the time. They intercede for themselves and others by binding, rebuking, and taking authority over the enemy through faith and prayer. A prayer warrior is someone who understands the power of prayer and the authority Christ has given us and operates in faith and courage to do battle against spiritual forces of darkness.

I mentioned at the conclusion of a previous chapter that there are several methods people use to help them establish a strong and consistent prayer life. We're going to look at a few of them now in an effort to help you do the same.

Pray without ceasing

You have seen this verse sprinkled throughout the pages of this book and here it is again: *Pray without ceasing. ~1st Thessalonians 5:17* Your mom always told you that practice makes perfect when it came time to practice your music lessons, or learn your multiplication facts. Well, the same holds true for the discipline of prayer. Practice makes perfect. The more you pray the more you will want to pray and the more you want to pray the more reliant you will become on God. And that, my friend, is about as perfect as it gets this side of heaven.

ACTS Acronym

Adoration: Giving God the glory, praise and honor due Him. Praising God for creation and for His forever-ness.

- *Who being the brightness of his glory, and the express image of his person, and upholding all things by the word of his power, when he had by himself purged our sins, sat down on the right hand of the Majesty on high: ~Hebrews 1:3*
- *And every creature which is in heaven, and on the earth, and under the earth, and such as are in the sea, and all that are in them, heard I saying, Blessing, and honour, and glory, and power, be unto him that sitteth upon the throne, and unto the Lamb for ever and ever. ~Revelation 5:13*
- *And thou shalt love the Lord thy God with all thy heart, and with all thy soul, and with all thy mind, and with all thy strength: this is the first commandment. ~Mark 12:30*

- *Praise ye the Lord. Praise God in his sanctuary: praise him in the firmament of his power. Praise him for his mighty acts: praise him according to his excellent greatness. Praise him with the sound of the trumpet: praise him with the psaltery and harp. Praise him with the timbrel and dance: praise him with stringed instruments and organs. Praise him upon the loud cymbals: praise him upon the high sounding cymbals. Let every thing that hath breath praise the Lord. Praise ye the Lord. ~Psalm 150*

Confession: Confessing your sins to God specifically, humbly, and with a heart of true repentance.

- *If we confess our sins, he is faithful and just to forgive us our sins, and to cleanse us from all unrighteousness. ~1st John 1:9*
- *He that covereth his sins shall not prosper: but whoso confesseth and forsaketh them shall have mercy. ~Proverbs 28:13*

- *Submit yourselves therefore to God. Resist the devil, and he will flee from you. Draw nigh to God, and he will draw nigh to you. Cleanse your hands, ye sinners; and purify your hearts, ye double minded. Be afflicted, and mourn, and weep: let your laughter be turned to mourning, and your joy to heaviness. Humble yourselves in the sight of the Lord, and he shall lift you up. ~James 4:7-10*
- *Have mercy upon me, O God, according to thy lovingkindness: according unto the multitude of thy tender mercies blot out my transgressions. Wash me throughly from mine iniquity, and cleanse me from my sin. For I acknowledge my transgressions: and my sin is ever before me. ~Psalm 51:1-3*

Thanksgiving: Give thanks to God for His blessings, His love, His mercy, His gift of salvation, and for the hope of heaven.

- *Giving thanks always for all things unto God and the Father in the name of our Lord Jesus Christ; ~Ephesians 5:20*
- *O give thanks unto the God of heaven: for his mercy endureth for ever. ~Psalm 136:26*
- *Bless the Lord, O my soul, and forget not all his benefits... ~Psalm 103:2*
- *Enter into his gates with thanksgiving, and into his courts with praise: be thankful unto him, and bless his name. ~Psalm 100:4*

Supplication: Praying on behalf of others and asking for the things we need and desire is definitely a part of prayer. Remember: prayer is communicating with God for the purpose of developing a deeper relationship with Him. That cannot happen if we aren't honest with God and if we don't open ourselves up completely to Him.

- *And this is the confidence that we have in him, that, if we ask any thing according to his will, he heareth us... ~1ˢᵗ John 5:14*
- *Ye ask, and receive not, because ye ask amiss, that ye may consume it upon your lusts. ~James 4:3*
- *But let him ask in faith, nothing wavering. For he that wavereth is like a wave of the sea driven with the wind and tossed. For let not that man think that he shall receive any thing of the Lord. A double minded man is unstable in all his ways. ~James 1:6-8*
- *My help cometh from the Lord, which made heaven and earth. ~Psalm 121:2*
- *Come unto me, all ye that labour and are heavy laden, and I will give you rest. ~Matthew 11:28*
- *And the Lord turned the captivity of Job, when he prayed for his friends: also the Lord gave Job twice as much as he had before. ~Job 42:10*

PRAY Acronym

The PRAY acronym is another often-used method of developing good prayer habits. As you can see, it is quite similar to the ACTS acronym, but then why wouldn't it be? They all follow the model prayer (the LORD's prayer) in Matthew 6.

There is, however, one aspect of the PRAY acronym I think needs to be highlighted. It is the Y, which reminds us to yield to God's purpose for our lives. So while I won't take the time to repeat every scripture used above for the ACTS acronym, I will insert a few of them in the appropriate place then focus on some that deal with yielding to God's will.

Praise: Giving God the glory, praise and honor due Him. Praising God for creation and for His forever-ness.

- *Who being the brightness of his glory, and the express image of his person, and upholding all things by the word of his power, when he had by himself purged our sins, sat down on the right hand of the Majesty on high: ~Hebrews 1:3*
- *And every creature which is in heaven, and on the earth, and under the earth, and such as are in the sea, and all that are in them, heard I saying, Blessing, and honour, and glory, and power, be unto him that sitteth upon the throne, and unto the Lamb for ever and ever. ~Revelation 5:13*

Repent: To repent means to change your ways. It is a reversing of yourself from living a sinful lifestyle to a Godly lifestyle.

- *And the times of this ignorance God winked at; but now commandeth all men every where to repent... Acts 17:30*

- *Know ye not that the unrighteous shall not inherit the kingdom of God? Be not deceived: neither fornicators, nor idolaters, nor adulterers, nor effeminate, nor abusers of themselves with mankind, nor thieves, nor covetous, nor drunkards, nor revilers, nor extortioners, shall inherit the kingdom of God. ~1st Corinthians 6:9-10*
- *Then Peter said unto them, Repent, and be baptized every one of you in the name of Jesus Christ for the remission of sins, and ye shall receive the gift of the Holy Ghost. ~Acts 2:38*
- *And be not conformed to this world: but be ye transformed by the renewing of your mind, that ye may prove what is that good, and acceptable, and perfect, will of God. ~Romans 12:2*

- *And fear not them which kill the body, but are not able to kill the soul: but rather fear him which is able to destroy both soul and body in hell. ~Matthew 10:28*

Ask: Asking God for the desires of your heart, for the needs you have in your life, and for the provision and safety for others all comes under this 'category'.

- *Ye ask, and receive not, because ye ask amiss, that ye may consume it upon your lusts. ~James 4:3*
- *But let him ask in faith, nothing wavering. For he that wavereth is like a wave of the sea driven with the wind and tossed. For let not that man think that he shall receive any thing of the Lord. A double minded man is unstable in all his ways. ~James 1:6-8*
- *My help cometh from the Lord, which made heaven and earth. ~Psalm 121:2*

- *Come unto me, all ye that labour and are heavy laden, and I will give you rest. ~Matthew 11:28*

Yield: To yield is to give in—to allow God to have His way in your life. Yielding is submission and obedience. Yielding is also living by faith.

- *For God so loved the world, that he gave his only begotten Son, that whosoever believeth in him should not perish, but have everlasting life. ~John 3:16*
- *What? know ye not that your body is the temple of the Holy Ghost which is in you, which ye have of God, and ye are not your own? ~1st Corinthians 6:19*
- *Trust in the Lord with all thine heart; and lean not unto thine own understanding. In all thy ways acknowledge him, and he shall direct thy paths. Be not wise in thine own eyes: fear the Lord, and depart from evil. ~Proverbs 3:5-7*

- *But be ye doers of the word, and not hearers only, deceiving your own selves. For if any be a hearer of the word, and not a doer, he is like unto a man beholding his natural face in a glass: For he beholdeth himself, and goeth his way, and straightway forgetteth what manner of man he was. But whoso looketh into the perfect law of liberty, and continueth therein, he being not a forgetful hearer, but a doer of the work, this man shall be blessed in his deed. ~James 1:22-25*
- *Be ye therefore followers of God, as dear children. ~Ephesians 5:1*
- *For if we sin wilfully after that we have received the knowledge of the truth, there remaineth no more sacrifice for sins, But a certain fearful looking for of judgment and fiery indignation, which shall devour the adversaries. ~Hebrews 10:26-27*
- *God is a Spirit: and they that worship him must worship him in spirit and in truth. ~John 4:24*

I'll say it again: a prayer warrior is someone who understands, believes in, and depends on the power of prayer. Be a prayer warrior!

Chapter 9:

Praying for Healing

Praying for the healing of self and others is something many of us have difficulty in wrapping our heads and hearts around. We pray believing God will hear us. We pray believing God will give us what we ask for because that is what scripture tells us. We pray, yet much of the time our prayers are not answered in the way we think they should be. Our loved one dies. An innocent child is taken from the loving arms of their parents. Soldiers don't come home.

So what's the matter? Are we praying wrong? Is the Bible lying?

The answers to those questions are as follows:

We may or may not be praying 'wrong'. While it is never wrong to ask God to heal someone so that we can continue to enjoy loving them here on earth or so that their families can remain intact, our first prayer should always be for God's will to be done because His will is always perfect and right. Secondly we can pray for those we wish to pray for, but along with those prayers we should ask God for the strength and wisdom necessary to accept His answer.

Right now a young family in the Midwest is praying earnestly for their infant son. He has a somewhat rare disease that has robbed him of his ability to swallow on his own, to sit or stand, and of the ability for his lungs to expel fluid. This little guy has to spend most of his time hooked to one machine or another. He will likely not reach his second birthday. His parents, grandparents, and countless friends, family, and other prayer warriors are praying for baby Logan and his family.

They are praying for miraculous healing. But they are also praying for strength, courage, and wisdom to give him the best of their love for whatever time God gives them together.

No, the Bible is not lying. The Bible tells us that whatever we ask for in God's will it will be done. Yet we have to remember God's will first - Always first.

Keeping that in mind, let's take a look at some of the scriptures dealing with prayers for healing. As you read them, think about how you can be more in tune to God's will and prayers for His children.

Most of all remember this: Healing in its best and truest form is to be with God the Father for all eternity. Not to sound morbid or anything but for those who are saved but dealing with terminal illness, healing is often physical death.

- *Is any among you afflicted? let him pray. Is any merry? let him sing psalms. Is any sick among you? let him call for the elders of the church; and let them pray over him, anointing him with oil in the name of the Lord: And the prayer of faith shall save the sick, and the Lord shall raise him up; and if he have committed sins, they shall be forgiven him. Confess your faults one to another, and pray one for another, that ye may be healed. The effectual fervent prayer of a righteous man availeth much. ~James 5:13-16*
- *And we know that all things work together for good to them that love God, to them who are the called according to his purpose. ~Romans 8:28*

- *Beloved, I wish above all things that thou mayest prosper and be in health, even as thy soul prospereth. ~3rd John 1:2*
- *Who his own self bare our sins in his own body on the tree, that we, being dead to sins, should live unto righteousness: by whose stripes ye were healed. ~1st Peter 2:24*

As I mentioned before when are prayers don't get answered, especially prayers for love ones healing it can cause confusion and doubt in your faith and sometimes even in God. Yet this is a snare of the devil to keep you locked in bondage – learn to break free from the oppression of the devil by walking in faith, encourage, and in the word of God. One way to break free from this oppression in bondage is to develop a checklist of sorts.

Consider the following is a short checklist:

- Is there sin in my life preventing my prayers from being answered
- Do I know for certain what I'm praying is God's will? – If not then pray that God's will would be done on earth as it is in heaven in the situation.
- I'm I being targeted by workers of darkness such as witches, Satanist, and others who practice the dark arts?
- Have I cleansed myself from all generational curses or familiar spirits?
- Is my relationship with God where it needs to be?
- Have I prayed over my house or place of continual prayer?
- Is there an open door that I or my family members have inadvertently opened to enable the spiritual forces of darkness to hinder my prayer life?
- Are there things in my home that are spiritually charged that are affecting my prayer life?
- Have I done my due diligence, and through the Spirit of God attempted to research and rightly divide the Word of God as it pertains to the specific situation?

These are just a few questions to ask yourself when you're prayers are not being answered. Sometimes it's also critical to fast and pray – remember it's a real war and it's here every day.

Chapter 10:

Praying as a Means of Spiritual Warfare

Spiritual Warfare sounds even scarier and more intimidating than the term 'Prayer Warrior'. That's because it can actually be a very scary thing if you don't know what you're doing or who you are in Christ Jesus. Learn from the clear example below in the Word of God not to try this unless you know who you are in Christ.

Acts 19:11-17

[11] Now God worked unusual miracles by the hands of Paul, [12] so that even handkerchiefs or aprons were brought from his body to the sick, and the diseases left them and the evil spirits went out of them. [13] Then some of the itinerant Jewish exorcists took it upon themselves to call the name of the Lord Jesus over those who had evil spirits, saying, "We exorcise you by the Jesus whom Paul preaches." [14] Also there were seven sons of Sceva, a Jewish chief priest, who did so.

[15] And the evil spirit answered and said, "Jesus I know, and Paul I know; but who are you?"

[16] Then the man in whom the evil spirit was leaped on them, overpowered them, and prevailed against them, so that they fled out of that house naked and wounded. [17] This became known both to all Jews and Greeks dwelling in Ephesus; and fear fell on them all, and the name of the Lord Jesus was magnified.

Now I'm not trying to scare you here but you have to understand there is a real war going on between the Kingdom of God and the kingdom of the devil. This is a spiritual war with earthly consequences. Fallen Angels, demons, and demonic possession are all very real things and is not something that the novice should get into with little to no training. One of the best men of God in our age to learn from is Russ Dizdar. His website is www.shatterthedarkness.com for those interested in learning more about his ministry.

We don't need to be scared of the devil but mindful of his ways and unrelenting attacks on our hearts, souls, minds, and bodies.

⁸ Be sober, be vigilant; because your adversary the devil walks about like a roaring lion, seeking whom he may devour. ⁹ Resist him, steadfast in the faith, knowing that the same sufferings are experienced by your brotherhood in the world - 1 Peter 5:8-9

[11] lest Satan should take advantage of us; for we are not ignorant of his devices - 2 Cor. 2:11

[7] Therefore submit to God. Resist the devil and he will flee from you. – James 4:7

We don't need to be afraid of what the devil can do to us, we have been given authority over him and all his evil minions. We don't need to even be afraid of being separated from God somehow either here on earth or for all eternity. Let's let the Scriptures speak for themselves, below you can see that nothing can separate us from the love of God in Christ Jesus in addition to Christ giving us all authority to trample on serpents and scorpions and over all the power of the enemy – did you see the word all. That sounds pretty absolute to me. The main thing that we need to realize here is what manner of spirit we are of – 2 Tim 1:7 makes it very clear that God has not given us a spirit of fear, but of power, and of love, and of a sound mind.

^{38} For I am persuaded that neither death nor life, nor angels nor principalities nor powers, nor things present nor things to come, ^{39} nor height nor depth, nor any other created thing, shall be able to separate us from the love of God which is in Christ Jesus our Lord -Rom. 8:38-39

^{4} You are of God, little children, and have overcome them, because He who is in you is greater than he who is in the world -1 John 4:4

^{17} Then the seventy returned with joy, saying, "Lord, even the demons are subject to us in Your name." ^{18} And He said to them, "I saw Satan fall like lightning from heaven. ^{19} Behold, I give you the authority to trample on serpents and scorpions, and over all the power of the enemy, and nothing shall by any means hurt you. ^{20} Nevertheless do not rejoice in this, that the spirits are subject to you, but rather rejoice because your names are written in heaven - Luke 10: 17-20

[7] For God has not given us a spirit of fear, but of power and of love and of a sound mind 2 Tim 1:7

[18] There is no fear in love; but perfect love casts out fear, because fear involves torment. But he who fears has not been made perfect in love. 1 John 4:18

Spiritual warfare is very real. Look around you -the social unrest, the violence in our schools and in our streets, the persecution of Christians around the world (including here in the US), and the demoralizing of our society screams spiritual attacks from the devil and his minions. The devil is on the move and making great strides because he knows his time is short - *[7] And war broke out in heaven: Michael and his angels fought with the dragon; and the dragon and his angels fought, [8] but they did not prevail, nor was a place found for them in heaven any longer.*

⁹ So the great dragon was cast out, that serpent of old, called the Devil and Satan, who deceives the whole world; he was cast to the earth, and his angels were cast out with him. ¹⁰ Then I heard a loud voice saying in heaven, "Now salvation, and strength, and the kingdom of our God, and the power of His Christ have come, for the accuser of our brethren, who accused them before our God day and night, has been cast down. ¹¹ And they overcame him by the blood of the Lamb and by the word of their testimony, and they did not love their lives to the death. ¹²Therefore rejoice, O heavens, and you who dwell in them! ***Woe to the inhabitants of the earth and the sea! For the devil has come down to you, having great wrath, because he knows that he has a short time."*** *Rev. 12:7-12*

But know this: God has already won, He is Victorious. He has already Won the War and those who are in Christ have the Victory – IF They Claim It and Walk in It

Let these verses equip you for the battles to come:

- *For we wrestle not against flesh and blood, but against principalities, against powers, against the rulers of the darkness of this world, against spiritual wickedness in high places. ~Ephesians 6:12*
- *Above all, taking the shield of faith, wherewith ye shall be able to quench all the fiery darts of the wicked. ~Ephesians 6:16*
- *Be sober, be vigilant; because your adversary the devil, as a roaring lion, walketh about, seeking whom he may devour ~1st Peter 5:8*
- *Submit yourselves therefore to God. Resist the devil, and he will flee from you. ~James 4:7*
- *For whatsoever is born of God overcometh the world: and this is the victory that overcometh the world, even our faith. Who is he that overcometh the world, but he that believeth that Jesus is the Son of God? ~1st John 5:4-5*
- *No weapon that is formed against thee shall prosper; and every tongue that shall rise against thee in judgment thou shalt condemn. This is the heritage of the servants of the Lord, and their righteousness is of me, saith the Lord. ~Isaiah 54:17*

The Scriptures above are clear and to the point – we have the authority, we have the victory, we have everything we need to defeat the devil and everything he throws at us if we have the courage and the faith to believe God's Word enough to take action in our daily lives. Will you boldly walk out your faith today?

Praying for your enemies

Let's briefly discuss praying for your enemies. There are several reasons that if you're a follower of Jesus Christ should pray for your enemies. First and foremost we have to guard against hatred and resentment building up within our spirit. Hatred and resentment is like a spiritual cancer that infects our spirit separating us from completing God's perfect will for our life. There is a fundamental Christian principle that Christ taught us and that is to be forgiven we have to forgive others – it's just that simple.

A lot of times when we do not forgive someone, in all reality it's only affecting us - the other person probably has no clue of the entirety of your feelings.

Let's once again look to the Scripture for clarification:

Matt. 5:43-47

⁴³ "You have heard that it was said, 'You shall love your neighbor and hate your enemy.' ⁴⁴But I say to you, love your enemies, bless those who curse you, do good to those who hate you, and pray for those who spitefully use you and persecute you, ⁴⁵ that you may be sons of your Father in heaven; for He makes His sun rise on the evil and on the good, and sends rain on the just and on the unjust. ⁴⁶ For if you love those who love you, what reward have you? Do not even the tax collectors do the same? ⁴⁷ And if you greet your brethren only, what do you do more than others? Do not even the tax collectors do so? ⁴⁸ Therefore you shall be perfect, just as your Father in heaven is perfect.

Rom. 12:9-21

⁹ Let love be without hypocrisy. Abhor what is evil. Cling to what is good. ¹⁰ Be kindly affectionate to one another with brotherly love, in honor giving preference to one another; ¹¹ not lagging in diligence, fervent in spirit, serving the Lord; ¹² rejoicing in hope, patient in tribulation, continuing steadfastly in prayer; ¹³ distributing to the needs of the saints, given to hospitality.

¹⁴ Bless those who persecute you; bless and do not curse. ¹⁵ Rejoice with those who rejoice, and weep with those who weep. ¹⁶ Be of the same mind toward one another. Do not set your mind on high things, but associate with the humble. Do not be wise in your own opinion.

¹⁷ Repay no one evil for evil. Have regard for good things in the sight of all men. ¹⁸ If it is possible, as much as depends on you, live peaceably with all men. ¹⁹ Beloved, do not avenge yourselves, but rather give place to wrath; for it is written, "Vengeance is Mine, I will repay," says the Lord. ²⁰ Therefore

*"If your enemy is hungry, feed him;
If he is thirsty, give him a drink;
For in so doing you will heap coals of fire on his head."*

[21] Do not be overcome by evil, but overcome evil with good.

Releasing this type of hatred, resentment, and unforgiveness cleanses your spirit as you repent of these things and enables you to draw closer to God. Now this is not to say that there isn't a time and a place for righteous anger. The Bible declares that you can be angry and not sin but you have to be led by the Word of God and His Holy Spirit.

Chapter 11:

Developing Your Prayer List

What is a prayer list?

The simple definition of a prayer list according to yours truly is simply a list of items that you feel compelled to pray for – normally the items on this list are prayed for when I consistent basis every day until God puts it on your heart to move on to something else. For example praying for the salvation of a loved one by their specific name, or if a relative is dealing with a sickness or illness.

Getting Serious!

Developing a prayer list could potentially be one sign that you're starting to take prayer more serious.

It's an indication that you understand the power and the value of praying consistently each and every day to affect change in the dynamics you're dealing with. I found this to be true in my case. Sure I prayed as the Spirit led, or when there was a need but slowly the Holy Spirit put within my heart a burden for the salvation of my mother and other people around me and it was at this point that I started writing down things to pray for and putting it up where I could see it continually. See I'm a visual person and a lot of times if I don't see it I will forget it – I'm sure a lot of you can relate to this, especially with how hectic life can be.

Therefore, I cannot stress strongly enough that once you've created a prayer list that you put it up somewhere in which you will continually see it such as a home office. Oh – make sure you either write it large enough to see it or type it in a font that's large enough for you to see it from a distance.

The bottom line is just to keep it in front of you and in your mind. Don't let prayers go one prayed because of lack of discipline and spiritual laziness. To be a strong Christian prayer warrior requires discipline, vigilance, and the warrior spirit that the Lord himself will mold you into.

They Why

The Why is straightforward here. We all forget things, that's just a reality of life, don't beat yourself up about it just keep it moving ever adapting to changes and situations that the devil attempts to throw at you. As you continue to develop into a prayer warrior your intensity, passion, and desire to serve the living God will increase to the point where you will continually walk victorious – remember you are Christ's ambassadors, the King of Kings and the Lord of lords.

An Example of My Prayer List

In this section I want to share with you my personal prayer list. This is my general list of things that I pray for or about on a consistent basis. Please note the order in which I list them as there is a systematic order in which I pray from the first thing to the last thing (normally).

They are as follows:

- Giving Thanks – showing my appreciation for all that God is doing, has done, and will do
- Repentance - this is something I pray as needed
- Protection - pleading the blood of Jesus over me and my family and those around us
- Salvation - for my family members, neighbors, and specific people my life
- Healing - if there is a specific medical need, but at times I pray that salvation and healing walk hand-in-hand

- Revival - that God would stir the hearts and minds of his people
- Brothers and Sisters in Christ -for protection, healing, leading, for God's perfect will to be done in their lives
- For Leadership in Government - this includes America and Israel
- Workers for the harvest -this is praying the Scriptures -for God to send workers
- Prayer Warriors -for God to raise up Prayer Warriors
- Those Most Vulnerable in Our Society - in this area I pray for the elderly, the sick and affirmed, the homeless and hungry, those in foster care, those still within their mother's womb, and for the children worldwide to be protected. In this section I start to really get into spiritual warfare. I pray against the spiritual forces behind pedophile rings, Satanic networks, human trafficking networks, sex trafficking networks.

I pray that the Lord would send His angels – yes is holy and righteous Angels to protect every single person in our society without a voice who may be being abused, tortured, molested, or maybe they have been kidnapped, and may soon be sacrificed to the enemy. Then ask God specifically to help us and the systematic murder of the children that are still yet in her mother's womb – this Holocaust, this bloodshed has to come to an end if our nation has any chance for redemption. Because understand this this bloodshed is literally part of sacrifices to the devil. Many people don't understand that blood is a currency in the amount of innocent blood that has been shed is overwhelming – help me pray against this brothers and sisters. Through prayer we can shine God's light into the darkness was focus our efforts together in prayer and shine God's light into the darkness to expose this evil and abolish it from our land.

- Against the Enemy - after I've begun to pray for those most vulnerable in our society and against the demonic forces that seek to destroy them I then shift gears and specifically go after the spiritual enemy even more.

Chapter 12:

When It Seems God Doesn't Hear Your Prayers

When God Doesn't Answer Prayers?

We've touched on this already to some degree but let's examine some times in Scripture were men of "Faith" don't have their prayers answered or answered immediately.

- Daniel - Prince of Persia holding him up
- The Disciples of Jesus – Faithless, Perversion, Jesus said, "Because of your unbelief"

- Job - A perfect example of following God faithfully and having sudden destruction fall upon you similar to the way we may pray but not necessarily see an answer to our prayers. God allowed Satan to attack Job and his family – but what you see here is that whatever is happening God is still in charge. Satan had to come and get God's permission to do anything to Job. So even though times may seem dark you are still in the palm of his hand if you faithfully abide in Christ.
- The question you should ask yourself is this – Are you just honoring God with your mouth but your heart is far from Him?

This people draweth nigh unto me with their mouth, and honoureth me with their lips; but their heart is far from me. Matt. 15:8

Dan. 10:12-13

¹² Then said he unto me, Fear not, Daniel: for from the first day that thou didst set thine heart to understand, and to chasten thyself before thy God, thy words were heard, and I am come for thy words. ¹³ But the prince of the kingdom of Persia withstood me one and twenty days: but, lo, Michael, one of the chief princes, came to help me; and I remained there with the kings of Persia.

Matt. 17:15-21

¹⁵ Lord, have mercy on my son: for he is lunatick, and sore vexed: for ofttimes he falleth into the fire, and oft into the water. ¹⁶ And I brought him to thy disciples, and they could not cure him. ¹⁷ Then Jesus answered and said, O faithless and perverse generation, how long shall I be with you? how long shall I suffer you? bring him hither to me.

[18] And Jesus rebuked the devil; and he departed out of him: and the child was cured from that very hour. [19] Then came the disciples to Jesus apart, and said, Why could not we cast him out? [20] And Jesus said unto them, Because of your unbelief: for verily I say unto you, If ye have faith as a grain of mustard seed, ye shall say unto this mountain, Remove hence to yonder place; and it shall remove; and nothing shall be impossible unto you. [21] Howbeit this kind goeth not out but by prayer and fasting

Chapter 13:

Fasting and Prayer

If you want to really get serious about prayer than there's no better way than to add fasting to your prayer life. Fasting and prayer can be found throughout both the Old Testament and the New Testament. Fasting and prayer are normally related to drawling close to God and seeking a breakthrough in a particular situation. Let's take a look at some examples of fasting and prayer in the Bible.

Ezra 8: 21-22

[21] Then **I proclaimed a fast** there at the river of Ahava, **that we might humble ourselves before our God, to seek from Him the right way for us and our little ones and all our possessions.** [22] For I was ashamed to request of the king an escort of soldiers and horsemen to help us against the enemy on the road, because we had spoken to the king, saying, "The hand of our God *is* upon all those for good who seek Him, but His power and His wrath *are* against all those who forsake Him."

In Ezra we can see that the purpose of fasting and praying was to humble their cells before God and to seek God's direction for them and their families. I'm sure many of us can relate to wanting to know what the right path is.

We can see from Scripture that fasting and praying is a way for us to humble ourselves, lean not unto her own understanding, and seek God's direction for our lives. How many of us can truly say that we have done this? Draw close to God and he will draw close to you and you will know your path.

Psalms 35:11-14

[11] Fierce witnesses rise up; They ask me *things* that I do not know. [12] They reward me evil for good, *To* the sorrow of my soul. [13] But as for me, when they were sick, My clothing *was* sackcloth; I humbled myself with fasting; And my prayer would return to my own heart. [14] I paced about as though *he were* my friend *or* brother; I bowed down heavily, as one who mourns *for his* mother.

In Psalms 35 we again see fasting as a way to humble ourselves before God Almighty. We can also see that prayer comes from the heart. The Scriptures declare, "Out of the abundance of the heart the mouth speaks" – (Matt. 12:34 / Luke 6:45) is a critical spiritual principle or law if you would – for in the power of the tongue there is life and there is death (Proverbs 18:21), speak life! Speak life to your situations, circumstances and call those things that are not as if they are according to the word of God – this is the essence of faith.

- Now **faith is the** substance of things hoped for, **the evidence** of things not seen (Heb. 11:13)
- [6] But without faith it is impossible to please him: for he that cometh to God must believe that he is, and that he is a rewarder of them that diligently seek him (Heb. 11:6).

- [27] And Jesus looking upon them saith, With men it is impossible, but not with God: for with God all things are possible (Mark 10:27)
- [11] Not that I speak in respect of want: for I have learned, in whatsoever state I am, therewith to be content. [12] I know both how to be abased, and I know how to abound: every where and in all things I am instructed both to be full and to be hungry, both to abound and to suffer need. [13] I can do all things through Christ which strengtheneth me (Philippians 4:11-13)

Daniel 9:2-22

² In the first year of his reign I, Daniel, understood by the books the number of the years *specified* by the word of the Lord through Jeremiah the prophet, that He would accomplish seventy years in the desolations of Jerusalem.

³ Then **I set my face toward the Lord God to make request by prayer and supplications, with fasting, sackcloth, and ashes**. ⁴ And I prayed to the Lord my God, and made confession, and said, "O Lord, great and awesome God, who keeps His covenant and mercy with those who love Him, and with those who keep His commandments, ⁵ we have sinned and committed iniquity, we have done wickedly and rebelled, even by departing from Your precepts and Your judgments.

⁶ Neither have we heeded Your servants the prophets, who spoke in Your name to our kings and our princes, to our fathers and all the people of the land. ⁷ O Lord, righteousness *belongs* to You, but to us shame of face, as *it is* this day—to the men of Judah, to the inhabitants of Jerusalem and all Israel, those near and those far off in all the countries to which You have driven them, because of the unfaithfulness which they have committed against You. ⁸ "O Lord, to us *belongs* shame of face, to our kings, our princes, and our fathers, because we have sinned against You. ⁹ To the Lord our God *belong* mercy and forgiveness, though we have rebelled against Him. ¹⁰ We have not obeyed the voice of the Lord our God, to walk in His laws, which He set before us by His servants the prophets.

¹¹ Yes, all Israel has transgressed Your law, and has departed so as not to obey Your voice; therefore the curse and the oath written in the Law of Moses the servant of God have been poured out on us, because we have sinned against Him. ¹² And He has confirmed His words, which He spoke against us and against our judges who judged us, by bringing upon us a great disaster; for under the whole heaven such has never been done as what has been done to Jerusalem. ¹³ "As *it is* written in the Law of Moses, all this disaster has come upon us; yet we have not made our prayer before the Lord our God, that we might turn from our iniquities and understand Your truth. ¹⁴ Therefore the Lord has kept the disaster in mind, and brought it upon us; for the Lord our God *is* righteous in all the works which He does, though we have not obeyed His voice.

[15] And now, O Lord our God, who brought Your people out of the land of Egypt with a mighty hand, and made Yourself a name, as *it is* this day—we have sinned, we have done wickedly!

[16] O Lord, according to all Your righteousness, I pray, let Your anger and Your fury be turned away from Your city Jerusalem, Your holy mountain; because for our sins, and for the iniquities of our fathers, Jerusalem and Your people *are* a reproach to all *those* around us. [17] Now therefore, our God, hear the prayer of Your servant, and his supplications, and for the Lord's sake cause Your face to shine on Your sanctuary, which is desolate.

[18] O my God, incline Your ear and hear; open Your eyes and see our desolations, and the city which is called by Your name; for we do not present our supplications before You because of our righteous deeds, but because of Your great mercies. [19] O Lord, hear! O Lord, forgive! O Lord, listen and act! Do not delay for Your own sake, my God, for Your city and Your people are called by Your name." [20] Now while I *was* speaking, praying, and confessing my sin and the sin of my people Israel, and presenting my supplication before the Lord my God for the holy mountain of my God, [21] yes, while I *was* speaking in prayer, the man Gabriel, whom I had seen in the vision at the beginning, being caused to fly swiftly, reached me about the time of the evening offering. [22] And he informed *me,* and talked with me, and said, "O Daniel, I have now come forth to give you skill to understand.

The Scripture in Daniel 9 is a great example of how to pray for your country. Though God was talking specifically to Solomon regarding the house of the Lord we can see from Daniel chapter 9 that Daniel still prayed according to 2 Chon. 7:14. I'm sure a lot of you reading this book probably know the Scripture by heart but how many of us have fasted and prayed like Daniel to seek a healing for the land. Understand to heal the land requires that each of us are healed ourselves internally and spiritually.

- [14] If my people, which are called by my name, shall humble themselves, and pray, and seek my face, and turn from their wicked ways; then will I hear from heaven, and will forgive their sin, and will heal their land - (2 Chron. 7:14).

Matthew 17:20-21 Mark 9:28-29

[20] And Jesus said unto them, Because of your unbelief: for verily I say unto you, If ye have faith as a grain of mustard seed, ye shall say unto this mountain, Remove hence to yonder place; and it shall remove; and nothing shall be impossible unto you. [21] Howbeit this kind goeth not out but by prayer and fasting.

As we can see without faith you will have no victory in spiritual warfare. And remember, without faith it is impossible to please God – the One who enlisted you in His army. But make no mistake about it we will endure hardship as a good soldier of Jesus Christ according to Scripture –(2 Tim 2:3).

However, hardship is not defeat it is just merely part of the war that were all in and some battles leave us more wounded than others. Nevertheless we have the victory in Christ regardless of how wounded we get.

Having the proper mindset is critical and this mindset comes from transforming yourself into the word of God, not the Word of God transforming itself into today's societal norms. Remember, heaven and earth will pass away but God's Word will remain the same – (Matt. 24:35).

It's important that we don't get discouraged in the battle, going back to the mindset once again.

Could you imagine the confusion of the apostles had when they attempted to invoke the name of Jesus and the demon wasn't cast out? Why did this happen? Jesus says this happen because of two things – their unbelief and the fact that this particular type of demon only comes out through fasting and prayer. I would speculate that because of the fierceness of this particular demon, because the apostles believe the lie of the physical world, of what they saw they were moved in their heart to believe that this demon is too strong. I believe this is the essence of where their unbelief stemmed from.

Now this is just speculation based off of reading the Scriptures no one can be entirely sure where of their unbelief stemmed from but it did originate from somewhere.

Additionally Jesus indicated that this particular type of demon only comes out through fasting and prayer. Now was He specifically talking regarding the apostles because of their unbelief or can this be universally applied? I tend to look at it like this – because of the apostles unbelief they needed to humble themselves before God by fasting and then pray for the demon to be removed. Because the Scriptures very clearly tell us that Christ has given us all authority over the enemy.

Let's review this real quick:

- Then He called His twelve disciples together and gave them power and authority over **all demons**, and to cure diseases. [2] He sent them to preach the kingdom of God and to heal the sick - (Luke 9:1-2)

- ¹⁸ And He said to them, "I saw Satan fall like lightning from heaven. ¹⁹ Behold, I give you the authority to trample on serpents and scorpions, **and over all the power of the enemy**, and nothing shall by any means hurt you. ²⁰ Nevertheless do not rejoice in this, that the spirits are subject to you, but rather rejoice because your names are written in heaven." – (Luke 10:18-20).

The main thing to remember about the Scripture is to have faith, real faith and if you're struggling with faith pray and ask God to give you the faith that's needed to do his will each and every day. It's not just enough to know about God or to even read a book about God – you have to believe in your hearts and then confessed publicly with your mouth - (Rom 10:9-10).

Strongholds of the enemy may be present in your life or in a situation during which time is highly recommended if you want to have the victory over these things that you fast and pray.

Luke 2:36-38

36 And there was one Anna, a prophetess, the daughter of Phanuel, of the tribe of Aser: she was of a great age, and had lived with an husband seven years from her virginity; 37 And she was a widow of about fourscore and four years, which departed not from the temple, but served God with fastings and prayers night and day. 38 And she coming in that instant gave thanks likewise unto the Lord, and spake of him to all them that looked for redemption in Jerusalem.

Here we see a combination of a virtuous woman and a prayer warrior. The Scriptures indicate that she was a woman of honor who followed the word of God even after her husband's death. We can see her dedication to the Lord in the fact that she did not depart from the temple but served God with fastings and prayers both day and night all the meanwhile continuingly telling people where they can find redemption – a powerful woman of God.

Luke 5:33-35

[33] And they said unto him, Why do the disciples of John fast often, and make prayers, and likewise the disciples of the Pharisees; but thine eat and drink? [34] And he said unto them, Can ye make the children of the bridechamber fast, while the bridegroom is with them? [35] **But the days will come, when the bridegroom shall be taken away from them, and then shall they fast in those days.**

Brothers and sisters we are in the days Jesus spoke about, the days in which we shall fast and pray. When is the last time you fasted and prayed? If you're truly serious about being a prayer warrior, if you want to take your prayer life to the next level, if you want to draw close to God than it's time to start fasting and praying on a more regular basis.

Now obviously if you have specific medical needs or conditions it's important to consult with your primary doctor to ensure that it is safe for you to fast. If you do have medical conditions that preclude you from completely fasting then maybe consider a juice fast. A juice fast requires the use of a juicer that processes vegetables and fruits into pure juice without the pulp and the fiber.

This is a great way to get started with fasting because not only are you fasting from particular items that you would normally eat but you're also doing something that will promote the overall health and well-being of your body – the temple of the living God.

1 Cor 7:2-5

² Nevertheless, to avoid fornication, let every man have his own wife, and let every woman have her own husband. ³ Let the husband render unto the wife due benevolence: and likewise also the wife unto the husband. ⁴ The wife hath not power of her own body, but the husband: and likewise also the husband hath not power of his own body, but the wife. ⁵ **Defraud ye not one the other, except it be with consent for a time, that ye may give yourselves to fasting and prayer;** and come together again, that Satan tempt you not for your incontinency.

The above Scripture is very interesting when we understand that the two become one in the flesh (Matt.19:5 / Mark 10:8 / 1 Cor. 6:16 / Eph. 5:31). However, the fact that the two become one in the flesh does not mean they come together as one in the spirit. Though the two are one in the flesh it is clear that each one has to work out our own salvation with fear and trembling before the Lord – (Philippians 2:12)

Scripture indicates not to withhold the love that is due one another except with consent for a time that you may give yourself to fasting and prayer and then come together again. There are some key points that we should address here:

- First and foremost there needs to be permission given – an agreement prior to restraining from giving yourself to one another.

- Secondly there is a time that is indicated in the agreement whether it's a day a week, whatever it is it is verbally articulated and agreed to by both parties.
- The only time this is permitted is for fasting and prayer
- You must come together immediately following your fast and prayer to ensure you are not tempted.

Chapter 14: Conclusion

It's up to each one of us to actively get into the fight, or maybe more importantly realize there is a war going on spiritually and we are all in a battle for our very souls. For the scriptures declare to "Wherefore, my beloved, as ye have always obeyed, not as in my presence only, but now much more in my absence, work out your own salvation with fear and trembling - Philippians 2:12"

This is a real war in the Spiritual realm that continues to bleed over into the physical world. So many men and women of God aren't even in the fight because they refuse to address their sin and run to God for forgiveness, let me tell you now – "As long as there is breath in Your lungs there is Hope in God for Change" – AJF

We must all do what we can, when we can, as God enables us ... From personally getting right with God, to effectively leading, guiding and protecting your family, to even effecting your community, society, and ultimately the world. Christians have forgotten what the "Far Left" has not – That one person can make a difference in the world and united we become stronger.

Why have Christians forgotten this critical lesson from History – Do we not remember that 12 men (Christ and the 11 Apostles – I don't really count Judas) Changed the World. We as Christian need to walk in that same boldness that they have walked in, that same Spirit of Conviction, Compassion, and Love. There is a time for everything under heaven and as you draw close to Jesus Christ the Holy Spirit will continually lead and guide you. The Question is do you really have Faith –

If you really have Faith you will "Take Action for the Kingdom of God". I challenge you to examine if you are in fact in the faith and to walk courageously, yes boldly in the Word of God for His name's sake. If we want to all make America great again then it's going to have to start with a transformation of each of our hearts and the hearts of those that claim to follow Christ – and that starts with Prayer.

What does the Scriptures say, "If my people, which are called by my name, shall **humble themselves, and Pray**, and seek my face, and turn from their wicked ways; then will I hear from heaven, and will forgive their sin, and will heal their land. 2 Chronicles 7:14" The time is now – "Take Action for the Kingdom of God" and get about the Father's business for tomorrow is never promised.

"Think For Yourself and Learn

Directly From God"

If you've learned nothing else in reading this book you've learned that without prayer our spiritual lives are basically non-existent. We cannot know God if we do not speak to Him and listen to Him. We cannot speak or listen to Him if we do not pray. There is a major difference between knowing God and being known by God.

Before I end this I also want to leave you with this scriptural truth: God hears and answers each and every prayer we say. Silent or out loud. Big or small concerns. He hears and answers them all. His answers may not always be what we want, but they will always be what we need

God bless each and every one of you who have read this book - know that I pray for all You as my Brother or Sister in Christ and that you are Not Alone in the War and together we can make a difference.

Special Gift

God has a Gift for You!   The Plan of Salvation:

There is no formal prayer of salvation as many churches would have you believe, God's Word is very clear - there is only one way to get to the Father in heaven and that is through Jesus Christ (John 14:6). Jesus says that you must be born again to enter into heaven (John 3:3-5).

Salvation is simply the first step in building an open and honest relationship with God. We all have sinned and fall short, but there is Hope in Jesus Christ - Just cry out to God in sincerity and honesty asking for forgiveness and for Him to Save you, Sanctify you, and fill you with His Holy Spirit - Ask for His will to be done in your life on earth as it is in Heaven and That's it, now just keep it real with God.

A Warning:

The Christian walk is not an easy life on the surface. The Word of God says that we will be hated in all the world for Christ namesake (Matt. 24:9). The Bible says that in the last days are enemy prevail against us physically until Christ returns to save us (Dan 7:21, 22). Furthermore, we must endure hardship as a good soldier of Jesus Christ (2 Tim 2:3) and yet we are never alone in this, God promises us that He will never leave us nor forsake us if we believe in him (Matt.28:20).

In everything we go through we have the peace and joy of God which surpasses all understanding (Philp. 4:6-8) The Bible declares, "For I consider the sufferings of this present time are not worthy to be compared with the glory which shall be revealed in us". (Rom 8:18). However, in all these things we are more than conquerors through Jesus Christ (Rom. 8:37)

Stay In Contact

Our Contact Information

Stay in Contact with the American Christian Defense Alliance, Inc. Email Us though Our Website At: http://www.ACDAInc.Org

Join Our Mailing List

We also Greatly Appreciate You Signing Up For Our Mailing List and Providing a Good Rating and review for this Book. Your reviews help other people like yourself find this book on Amazon and benefit from its contents.

If You or Your Family have been Blessed by this book please let us know by dropping us a line through our website at http://acdainc.org

Find All Our Books

Our Books:

Parenting: How To Be A Great Parent And Raise Awesome Kids

Real Men Don't Make Promises: Understanding Oaths, Pacts, Covenants & Promises From A Biblical Perspective

Salvation for Your Unsaved Mom: 10 Things to Tell Your Mom Before She Dies

The Perfection of Purity: A Message To My Daughter

A Vague Notion: How To Overcome Limiting Beliefs of Fear and Anxiety Through the Word of God

Biblical Bug Out: Don't Bug In - Follow The Calling

Christian Prepping 101: How To Start Prepping

Martial Arts Ministry: How To Start A Martial Arts Ministry

Bible Studies for Belts: A Guide for Christian Martial Arts, Vol. 1: White Belt

Prepping: Survival Basics

How to Finance Your Full-Time RV Dream

www.ingramcontent.com/pod-product-compliance
Lightning Source LLC
Chambersburg PA
CBHW032123160426
43197CB00008B/493